BIBLE 1000

Teacher's Guide

Author:
Alpha Omega Staff

Editor:
Alan Christopherson, M.S.

804 N. 2nd Ave. E.
Rock Rapids, IA 51246-1759

BIBLE 1000

LIFEPAC® Overview

BIBLE SCOPE & SEQUENCE

	Grade 1	Grade 2	Grade 3
UNIT 1	GOD CREATED ALL THINGS • God created day and night • God created land and sea • God created plants and animals • God created people	WHO AM I? • God made us • God loves me • God helps me • God helped Daniel	LIVING FOR GOD • I love and obey God • I praise God • I worship God • I serve God
UNIT 2	GOD LOVES HIS CHILDREN • God cared for Shadrach, Meshach, and Abednego • God cared for Joash and Esther • God cares for his children • God's children love him	THE STORY OF MOSES • The early life of Moses • Life in Midian • Moses returns to Egypt • Life in the desert	THE LIFE OF JESUS • Mary and Joseph • Jesus in the Temple • Jesus teaches and saves • Jesus dies and lives again
UNIT 3	WE CAN PRAY • We can ask and thank God • We can pray God's special prayer • God listens to us • We listen to God	GOD AND YOU • God is great • God keeps his promises • You should obey God • God rewards his people	GOD'S PLAN FOR JOSEPH • The dream of Joseph • Joseph and his brothers • Joseph in Egypt • God watched over Joseph
UNIT 4	GOD WANTS YOU TO BE GOOD • Jesus says love God • God says to love others • You show your love • God says to love yourself	HOW THE BIBLE CAME TO US • Moses and the Prophets • David and Solomon • The Apostles and Paul • Bible translators	YOU CAN USE THE BIBLE • The books of the Bible • How to read and study the Bible • How to find verses • How to memorize verses
UNIT 5	OLD TESTAMENT STORIES • Joseph, Elijah, Jonathan, and David • Miriam and Deborah • A rich woman and her son • Ishmael and Mephibosheth	DAVID'S SLING • David with the sheep • David and the prophet • David and Saul • David and the giant	GOD CARES FOR HIS PEOPLE • God's love for people • God guides people • God protects people • God blesses people
UNIT 6	GOD'S PROMISE • God's Old Testament promises • God's promises kept • The birth of the Promised One • The life of the Promised One	GOD IS EVERYWHERE • Understanding the beginning • Understanding God • The creation • God's will	THE BIBLE IS GOD'S WORD • The writers of God's Word • God's Word is preserved • God's Word changes lives • Promises of God's Word
UNIT 7	JESUS, OUR SAVIOR • Jesus taught the people • Jesus healed the people • Jesus saves the people • Jesus will come again	THE STORY OF JOSEPH • Joseph as a boy at home • The worship of Joseph • Joseph in Egypt • Joseph and the famine	ARCHAEOLOGY AND THE BIBLE • The search for treasure • Clues from old stories • Explaining the puzzles • Joining the search
UNIT 8	GOD CALLS MISSIONARIES • The woman at the well • Stephen and Paul • Missionaries today • God calls missionaries	GOD AND THE FAMILY • The first family • Abraham's family • Happy families • God's promise to children	GOD GAVE US THE NEED FOR FRIENDS • We need love • We need friendship • God commands our love • Love for others
UNIT 9	NEW TESTAMENT STORIES • Lazarus, Thomas, Stephen • Mary, Anna, Lydia • Children in the New Testament • Jesus and the children	GOD MADE THE NATIONS • The people of Babel • God's judgment at Babel • The new nation • Our big world	GOD'S PEOPLE HELP OTHERS • All people are created by God • God loves me • God's love to others • God is my Father
UNIT 10	GOD GAVE YOU MANY GIFTS • God created all things • God loves his children • God gave us his Word • God gave us his Son	GOD, HIS WORD, AND YOU • God as our Father • The Word of God • Life with God • Belonging to God	GOD'S WORD, JESUS, AND YOU • God speaks to Man • Writers of the Word • Jesus and the Word • God's family

BIBLE SCOPE & SEQUENCE

	Grade 4	Grade 5	Grade 6
UNIT 1	HOW CAN I LIVE FOR GOD? • Peter found Jesus • Peter fished for men • To be born into God's family • To be fruitful through the Spirit	HOW OTHERS LIVED FOR GOD • Fellow-laborers with God • Abraham, a man of faith • Servants of God • Co-workers with God	FROM CREATION TO MOSES • Creation • The Flood • Abraham and his descendants • Moses and the Law
UNIT 2	GOD'S KNOWLEDGE • Knowledge to create • Learning God's knowledge • The benefits of God's knowledge • Using God's knowledge	ANGELS • Characteristics of Angels • Kinds of Angels • The ministry of Angels • Angels in the life of Jesus	FROM JOSHUA TO SAMUEL • Conquest and division of the land • The death of Joshua • The Judges of Israel • Ruth, Naomi, and Boaz
UNIT 3	SAUL BEGINS TO LIVE FOR GOD • Saul persecutes the Christians • God changes Saul • Saul preaches about Jesus • Paul belongs to Christ	THE PRESENCE OF GOD • Everywhere as God • Everywhere as a person • In the lives of people • In my life	THE KINGDOM OF ISRAEL • Samuel and Saul • The reign of David • The reign of Solomon • The books of poetry
UNIT 4	THE BIBLE AND ME • Reading and learning the Bible • Thinking about the Bible • Memorizing the Bible • Living the Bible way	BIBLE METHODS AND STRUCTURE • One book with many parts • Books of history • Books of poetry and prophecy • Books of the New Testament	THE DIVIDED KINGDOM • From Jeroboam to Captivity • Prophets of Judah and Israel • From Hezekiah to Captivity • Prophets of remaining kingdom
UNIT 5	GOD CARES FOR US • The Twenty-third Psalm • Jesus and the sheep • David as a shepherd • Daniel as a helper	THE CHRISTIAN IN THE WORLD • Instruction and correction • Learning correct behavior • Relationships at school • Relationships in the world	CAPTIVITY AND RESTORATION • The prophets of the Captivity • The returns from exile • The prophets of the Restoration • Creation to Restoration
UNIT 6	HOW CAN I KNOW GOD EXISTS • God's plan for the Jews • A Jewish Savior • Man searches for God • Man needs God	PROVING WHAT WE BELIEVE • The Bible is God's Word • Evidence from the Bible • Evidence from history and science • Knowing that Christ arose	THE LIFE OF JESUS • Birth and background • The first years of ministry • The latter years of ministry • The death and Resurrection
UNIT 7	GEOGRAPHY OF THE OLD TESTAMENT • Bible geography • Description of the land • Abram's nomadic life • Abraham's descendants	MISSIONARY JOURNEYS OF PAUL • Paul's background • Paul's missionary journeys • The Jerusalem Council • Paul's last years	THE FOLLOWERS OF JESUS • The disciples of Jesus • The friends of Jesus • Miracles of Jesus • The message of Jesus
UNIT 8	GOD-GIVEN WORTH • Who Am I? • God is my Creator • God is my Father • Knowing God's love	GOD CREATED MAN FOR ETERNITY • Preparing for eternity • Christ is our Judge • The judgment of the Christian • The judgment of the unsaved	THE APOSTLE PAUL • Paul's background and conversion • Paul's missionary journeys • Paul's letters to churches • Paul's letters to people
UNIT 9	WITNESSING FOR JESUS • Loving God and others • Following Jesus • Knowing who Jesus is • Following Paul's example	AUTHORITY AND LAW • God is the source of law • The model of law • The authority of the family • Our authority of government	HEBREWS AND GENERAL EPISTLES • The book of Hebrews • James and 1st and 2nd Peter • The three Johns • The book of Jude
UNIT 10	GOD'S WAY IS PERFECT • Seeking knowledge • Science & geography • Living God's way • Loving God's way	ANGELS, THE BIBLE, LIVING FOR GOD • Presence of God and Angels • Understanding the Bible • Areas of service • The order of authority	REVELATION AND REVIEW • The Lord Jesus in Revelation • End-time events • Old Testament review • New Testament review

BIBLE SCOPE & SEQUENCE

	Grade 7	Grade 8	Grade 9
UNIT 1	WORSHIP • The nature of worship • Old Testament worship • New Testament worship • True worship	PRAYER • Organization of the Lord's Prayer • Purpose of the Lord's Prayer • History of prayer • Practical use of prayer	THE NEW TESTAMENT • Inter-Testamental period • Pharisees and Sadducees • New Testament themes • New Testament events
UNIT 2	MANKIND • The origin of man • The fall of man • The re-creation of man • The mission of man	SIN AND SALVATION • The nature of sin • The need for salvation • How to receive salvation • The results of salvation	THE GOSPELS • Matthew • Mark • Luke • John
UNIT 3	THE ATTRIBUTES OF GOD • God's nature of love • God's expression of love • The mercy of God • The grace of God	ATTRIBUTES OF GOD • God's justice • God's immutability • God's eternal nature • God's love	THE ACTS OF THE APOSTLES • The writer • The purpose • Pentecost • Missions
UNIT 4	FULFILLED PROPHECIES OF CHRIST • Method of the First Advent • Purpose of the First Advent • The Messiah foretold • Fulfillment of the Messiah	EARLY CHURCH LEADERS • The early church • The church of the Middle Ages • The Renaissance • The Reformation	THE PAULINE EPISTLES • Paul as a person • The early epistles • Prison epistles • The later epistles
UNIT 5	LIVING THE BALANCED LIFE • The Father's gift of life • Man's deception • Fellowship with the Savior • The life of the Spirit	EARLY CHURCH HISTORY • The Roman Empire • The background of the Jews • The ministry of Jesus • The Jerusalem church	GENERAL EPISTLES • James • First and Second Peter • First, Second, and Third John • Hebrews and Jude
UNIT 6	THE PSALMS • The history of the Psalms • Types of Psalms • Hebrew poetry • Psalm 100	THE EARLY CHURCHES • The church at Antioch • The missionary journeys • The Jerusalem Conference • New Testament churches	THE REVELATION OF JESUS CHRIST • The seven churches • The seven seals and trumpets • The seven signs and plagues • The seven judgments and wonders
UNIT 7	THE LIFE OF CHRIST: PART I • Early life of Christ • Christ's ministry begins • The early Judean ministry • The early Galilean ministry	THE BOOK OF PROVERBS • Literary forms and outline • Objectives and purposes • Influence on the New Testament • Key themes	JOB AND SUFFERING • The scenes of Job • Attitudes toward suffering • Christ's suffering on earth • The victory of Christ's suffering
UNIT 8	THE LIFE OF CHRIST: PART II • The public ministry in Galilee • The private ministry in Galilee • The Judean ministry • The Perean ministry	TODAY'S PROBLEMS • Guidance for behavior • Characteristics of friendship • Studying effectively • Finding God's will	HOW TO SHARE CHRIST • Personal evangelism • Outreach to others • Personal and family missions • Assisting a missionary
UNIT 9	THE LIFE OF CHRIST: PART III • The public Jerusalem ministry • The private Jerusalem ministry • The Crucifixion • The Resurrection	UNDERSTANDING PARENTS • Human parents • Biblical parents • Children's responsibility • Parents and children as a team	GOD'S WILL FOR MY LIFE • The desire of the heart • The Word and work of God • Importance of goals • The use of talents
UNIT 10	IN SUMMARY • The plan of God • Man's history • The Savior's solution • Worship of Christ	WALKING WITH GOD • Prayer and salvation • The attributes of God • The early church leaders • Christian living	THE WALK WITH CHRIST • Background of the New Testament • The Epistles and Revelation • The importance of suffering • God's will for my life

BIBLE SCOPE & SEQUENCE

	Grade 10	Grade 11	Grade 12
UNIT 1	CREATION TO ABRAHAM • The six days of creation • The fall of man • Noah and his descendants • Nations of the earth	THE FAITHFULNESS OF GOD • Affirmation of God's faithfulness • Nature of God's faithfulness • Manifestations of God's faithfulness • Implications of God's faithfulness	KNOWING YOURSELF • Your creation by God • Interacting with others • A child and servant of God • Your personal skills
UNIT 2	ABRAHAM TO MOSES • Abraham's call and promise • The covenant with Isaac • The life of Jacob • Joseph and his family	ROMANS: PART 1 • The Roman Empire and Church • The book of Romans • Paul's message to the Romans • Sin and salvation in Romans	CHRISTIAN MINISTRIES • Christian ministry defined • Church related ministries • Other ministries • A ministry as a career
UNIT 3	EXODUS AND WANDERINGS • The journey to Sinai • The giving of the Law • Numbering the people • The book of Deuteronomy	ROMANS: PART 2 • The chosen of God • Service and submission • From sin to salvation • The victory of salvation	CHOOSING A CHRISTIAN MINISTRY • Where to look for a ministry • What to look for in a ministry • How to look for a ministry • Choosing a ministry for a career
UNIT 4	ISRAEL IN CANAAN • Preparing for battle • The fight for the land • Dividing the land • The death of Joshua	THE DOCTRINE OF JESUS CHRIST • Identity and incarnation of Christ • The individuality of Christ • Christ's work on the Cross • Christ's work after the Cross	GODHEAD • Old Testament view • New Testament view • Historical Perspectives • Faith and man's relationship
UNIT 5	THE JUDGES AND SPIRITUAL DECLINE • Background of Judges • History of the Judges • Examples of spiritual decay • Ruth and redemption	THE NATION OF ISRAEL • The covenant with Abraham • Israel as a nation • Old Testament archaeology • New Testament archaeology	ATTRIBUTES OF GOD • The Holiness of God • The Goodness of God • Holiness and the believer • Goodness and the Creation
UNIT 6	THE KINGDOM • Samuel and Saul • David • Solomon • Hebrew poetry	HISTORY OF THE CANON • Revelation and inspiration • Illumination and interpretation • Authority of the Bible • Formation of the Bible	THE EPISTLES OF JAMES AND JOHN • James the man • The message of James • John the man • The message of John's epistles
UNIT 7	THE DIVIDED KINGDOM • Jeroboam to Ahab • Ahab to Jehu • Jehu to Assyrian Captivity • Prophets of the period	FRIENDSHIP, DATING, AND MARRIAGE • Meaning and role of friendship • Perspectives of dating • Principles of relationships • The structure of marriage	DANIEL • A man of conviction • An interpreter of dreams • A watchman in prayer • A man of visions
UNIT 8	THE REMAINING KINGDOM • The time of Hezekiah • Manasseh to Josiah • Jehoahaz to the exile • Prophets of the period	THE PURSUIT OF HAPPINESS • Solomon's succession • Solomon's prosperity • Solomon's fall • Solomon's reflection	COMPARATIVE RELIGIONS • Elements of Christianity • The validity of Christian faith • World religions • The occult
UNIT 9	THE CAPTIVITY • Prophets of the period • Jeremiah • Ezekiel • Daniel	ANSWERS FOR AGNOSTICS • Integrity of the Bible • Doctrines of the Bible • Interpretation of the Bible • Application of the Bible	WISDOM FOR TODAY'S YOUTH • Life and character of David • Life and riches of Solomon • Psalms and Proverbs • The Bible and literature
UNIT 10	THE RESTORATION • First return from exile • The Jews preserved • Second return from exile • Haggai, Zechariah, and Malachi	GOD, HIS WORD, AND THE CHRISTIAN • The uniqueness of the Bible • History of Israel • God revealed in the Bible • Principles for living	THE CHRISTIAN • Christian fundamentals • Growing in Christian maturity • A ministry for Christ • A testimony for Christ

STRUCTURE OF THE LIFEPAC CURRICULUM

The LIFEPAC curriculum is conveniently structured to provide one teacher's guide containing teacher support material with answer keys and ten student worktexts for each subject at grade levels 2 through 12. The worktext format of the LIFEPACs allows the student to read the textual information and complete workbook activities all in the same booklet. The easy-to-follow LIFEPAC numbering system lists the grade as the first number(s) and the last two digits as the number of the series. For example, the Language Arts LIFEPAC at the 6th grade level, 5th book in the series would be LAN0605.

Each LIFEPAC is divided into three to five sections and begins with an introduction or overview of the booklet as well as a series of specific learning objectives to give a purpose to the study of the LIFEPAC. The introduction and objectives are followed by a vocabulary section which may be found at the beginning of each section at the lower levels or in the glossary at the high school level. Vocabulary words are used to develop word recognition and should not be confused with the spelling words introduced later in the LIFEPAC. The student should learn all vocabulary words before working the LIFEPAC sections to improve comprehension, retention, and reading skills.

Each activity or written assignment in grades 2 through 12 has a number for easy identification, such as 1.1. The first number corresponds to the LIFEPAC section and the number to the right of the decimal is the number of the activity.

Teacher checkpoints, which are essential to maintain quality learning, are found at various locations throughout the LIFEPAC. The teacher should check 1) neatness of work and penmanship, 2) quality of understanding (tested with a short oral quiz), 3) thoroughness of answers (complete sentences and paragraphs, correct spelling, etc.), 4) completion of activities (no blank spaces), and 5) accuracy of answers as compared to the answer key (all answers correct).

The self test questions in grades 2 through 12 are also number coded for easy reference. For example, 2.015 means that this is the 15th question in the self test of Section 2. The first number corresponds to the LIFEPAC section, the zero indicates that it is a self test question, and the number to the right of the zero the question number.

The LIFEPAC test is packaged at the center of each LIFEPAC. It should be removed and put aside before giving the booklet to the student for study.

Answer and test keys in grades 2 through 12 have the same numbering system as the LIFEPACs. The student may be given access to the answer keys (not the test keys) under teacher supervision so that he can score his own work.

A thorough study of the Scope & Sequence by the teacher before instruction begins is essential to the success of the student. The teacher should become familiar with expected skill mastery and understand how these grade-level skills fit into the overall skill development of the curriculum. The teacher should also preview the objectives that appear at the beginning of each LIFEPAC for additional preparation and planning.

TEST SCORING AND GRADING

Answer keys and test keys give examples of correct answers. They convey the idea, but the student may use many ways to express a correct answer. The teacher should check for the essence of the answer, not for the exact wording. Many questions are high level and require thinking and creativity on the part of the student. Each answer should be scored based on whether or not the main idea written by the student matches the model example. "Any Order" or "Either Order" in a key indicates that no particular order is necessary to be correct.

Most self tests and LIFEPAC tests at the lower elementary levels are scored at 1 point per answer; however, the upper levels may have a point system awarding 2 to 5 points for various answers or questions. Further, the total test points will vary; they may not always equal 100 points. They may be 78, 85, 100, 105, etc.

Example 1

Example 2

A score box similar to ex. 1 above is located at the end of each self test and on the front of the LIFEPAC test. The bottom score, 72, represents the total number of points possible on the test. The upper score, 58, represents the number of points your student will need to receive an 80% or passing grade. If you wish to establish the exact percentage that your student has achieved, find the total points of his correct answers and divide it by the bottom number (in this case 72.) For example, if your student has a point total of 65, divide 65 by 72 for a grade of 90%. Referring to ex. 2, on a test with a total of 105 possible points, the student would have to receive a minimum of 84 correct points for an 80% or passing grade. If your student has received 93 points, simply divide the 93 by 105 for a percentage grade of 89%. Students who receive a score below 80% should review the LIFEPAC and retest using the appropriate Alternate Test found in the Teacher's Guide.

The following is a guideline to assign letter grades for completed LIFEPACs based on a maximum total score of 100 points.

Example:

LIFEPAC Test	=	60% of the Total Score (or percent grade)
Self Test	=	25% of the Total Score (average percent of self tests)
Reports	=	10% or 10* points per LIFEPAC
Oral Work	=	5% or 5* points per LIFEPAC

*Determined by the teacher's subjective evaluation of the student's daily work.

Example:

LIFEPAC Test Score	=	92%	92 x .60	= 55 points
Self Test Average	=	90%	90 x .25	= 23 points
Reports				= 8 points
Oral Work				= 4 points
TOTAL POINTS				= 90 points

Grade Scale based on point system:

100 – 94	=	A
93 – 86	=	B
85 – 77	=	C
76 – 70	=	D
Below 70	=	F

TEACHER HINTS AND STUDYING TECHNIQUES

LIFEPAC Activities are written to check the level of understanding of the preceding text. The student may look back to the text as necessary to complete these activities; however, a student should never attempt to do the activities without reading (studying) the text first. Self tests and LIFEPAC tests are never open book tests.

Language arts activities (skill integration) often appear within other subject curriculum. The purpose is to give the student an opportunity to test his skill mastery outside of the context in which it was presented.

Writing complete answers (paragraphs) to some questions is an integral part of the LIFEPAC Curriculum in all subjects. This builds communication and organization skills, increases understanding and retention of ideas, and helps enforce good penmanship. Complete sentences should be encouraged for this type of activity. Obviously, single words or phrases do not meet the intent of the activity, since multiple lines are given for the response.

Review is essential to student success. Time invested in review where review is suggested will be time saved in correcting errors later. Self tests, unlike the section activities, are closed book. This procedure helps to identify weaknesses before they become too great to overcome. Certain objectives from self tests are cumulative and test previous sections; therefore, good preparation for a self test must include all material studied up to that testing point.

The following procedure checklist has been found to be successful in developing good study habits in the LIFEPAC curriculum.

1. Read the introduction and Table of Contents.
2. Read the objectives.
3. Recite and study the entire vocabulary (glossary) list.
4. Study each section as follows:
    a. Read the introduction and study the section objectives.
    b. Read all the text for the entire section, but answer none of the activities.
    c. Return to the beginning of the section and memorize each vocabulary word and definition.
    d. Reread the section, complete the activities, check the answers with the answer key, correct all errors, and have the teacher check.
    e. Read the self test but do not answer the questions.
    f. Go to the beginning of the first section and reread the text and answers to the activities up to the self test you have not yet done.
    g. Answer the questions to the self test without looking back.
    h. Have the self test checked by the teacher.
    i. Correct the self test and have the teacher check the corrections.
    j. Repeat steps a–i for each section.
5. Use the SQ3R method to prepare for the LIFEPAC test.

    Scan the whole LIFEPAC.
    Question yourself on the objectives.
    Read the whole LIFEPAC again.
    Recite through an oral examination.
    Review weak areas.
6. Take the LIFEPAC test as a closed book test.
7. LIFEPAC tests are administered and scored under direct teacher supervision. Students who receive scores below 80% should review the LIFEPAC using the SQ3R* study method and take the Alternate Test located in the Teacher's Guide. The final test grade may be the grade on the Alternate Test or an average of the grades from the original LIFEPAC test and the Alternate Test.

GOAL SETTING AND SCHEDULES

Each school must develop its own schedule, because no single set of procedures will fit every situation. The following is an example of a daily schedule that includes the five LIFEPAC subjects as well as time slotted for special activities.

Possible Daily Schedule

8:15	-	8:25	Pledges, prayer, songs, devotions, etc.
8:25	-	9:10	Bible
9:10	-	9:55	Language Arts
9:55	-	10:15	Recess (juice break)
10:15	-	11:00	Math
11:00	-	11:45	History & Geography
11:45	-	12:30	Lunch, recess, quiet time
12:30	-	1:15	Science
1:15	-		Drill, remedial work, enrichment*

***Enrichment:** *Computer time, physical education, field trips, fun reading, games and puzzles, family business, hobbies, resource persons, guests, crafts, creative work, electives, music appreciation, projects.*

Basically, two factors need to be considered when assigning work to a student in the LIFEPAC curriculum.

The first is time. An average of 45 minutes should be devoted to each subject, each day. Remember, this is only an average. Because of extenuating circumstances, a student may spend only 15 minutes on a subject one day and the next day spend 90 minutes on the same subject.

The second factor is the number of pages to be worked in each subject. A single LIFEPAC is designed to take three to four weeks to complete. Allowing about three to four days for LIFEPAC introduction, review, and tests, the student has approximately 15 days to complete the LIFEPAC pages. Simply take the number of pages in the LIFEPAC, divide it by 15 and you will have the number of pages that must be completed on a daily basis to keep the student on schedule. For example, a LIFEPAC containing 45 pages will require three completed pages per day. Again, this is only an average. While working a 45-page LIFEPAC, the student may complete only one page the first day if the text has a lot of activities or reports, but go on to complete five pages the next day.

Long range planning requires some organization. Because the traditional school year originates in the early fall of one year and continues to late spring of the following year, a calendar should be devised that covers this period of time. Approximate beginning and completion dates can be noted on the calendar as well as special occasions such as holidays, vacations and birthdays. Since each LIFEPAC takes three to four weeks or 18 days to complete, it should take about 180 school days to finish a set of ten LIFEPACs. Starting at the beginning school date, mark off 18 school days on the calendar and that will become the targeted completion date for the first LIFEPAC. Continue marking the calendar until you have established dates for the remaining nine LIFEPACs making adjustments for previously noted holidays and vacations. If all five subjects are being used, the ten established target dates should be the same for the LIFEPACs in each subject.

TEACHING SUPPLEMENTS

The sample weekly lesson plan and student grading sheet forms are included in this section as teacher support materials and may be duplicated at the convenience of the teacher.

The student grading sheet is provided for those who desire to follow the suggested guidelines for assignment of letter grades as previously discussed. The student's self test scores should be posted as percentage grades. When the LIFEPAC is completed the teacher should average the self test grades, multiply the average by .25 and post the points in the box marked self test points. The LIFEPAC percentage grade should be multiplied by .60 and posted. Next, the teacher should award and post points for written reports and oral work. A report may be any type of written work assigned to the student whether it is a LIFEPAC or additional learning activity. Oral work includes the student's ability to respond orally to questions which may or may not be related to LIFEPAC activities or any type of oral report assigned by the teacher. The points may then be totaled and a final grade entered along with the date that the LIFEPAC was completed.

The Student Record Book, which was specifically designed for use with the Alpha Omega curriculum, provides space to record weekly progress for one student over a nine week period as well as a place to post self test and LIFEPAC scores. The Student Record Books are available through the current Alpha Omega catalog; however, unlike the enclosed forms these books are not for duplication and should be purchased in sets of four to cover a full academic year.

WEEKLY LESSON PLANNER

Week of:

	Subject	Subject	Subject	Subject
Monday				
	Subject	Subject	Subject	Subject
Tuesday				
	Subject	Subject	Subject	Subject
Wednesday				
	Subject	Subject	Subject	Subject
Thursday				
	Subject	Subject	Subject	Subject
Friday				

WEEKLY LESSON PLANNER

Week of:

	Subject	Subject	Subject	Subject
Monday				
	Subject	Subject	Subject	Subject
Tuesday				
	Subject	Subject	Subject	Subject
Wednesday				
	Subject	Subject	Subject	Subject
Thursday				
	Subject	Subject	Subject	Subject
Friday				

Student Name ______________________________ Year ______________

Bible

LP#	Self Test Scores by Sections					Self Test Points	LIFEPAC Test	Oral Points	Report Points	Final Grade	Date
	1	2	3	4	5						
01											
02											
03											
04											
05											
06											
07											
08											
09											
10											

History & Geography

LP#	Self Test Scores by Sections					Self Test Points	LIFEPAC Test	Oral Points	Report Points	Final Grade	Date
	1	2	3	4	5						
01											
02											
03											
04											
05											
06											
07											
08											
09											
10											

Language Arts

LP#	Self Test Scores by Sections					Self Test Points	LIFEPAC Test	Oral Points	Report Points	Final Grade	Date
	1	2	3	4	5						
01											
02											
03											
04											
05											
06											
07											
08											
09											
10											

Student Name ______________________ Year ______________

Math

LP#	Self Test Scores by Sections 1	2	3	4	5	Self Test Points	LIFEPAC Test	Oral Points	Report Points	Final Grade	Date
01											
02											
03											
04											
05											
06											
07											
08											
09											
10											

Science

LP#	Self Test Scores by Sections 1	2	3	4	5	Self Test Points	LIFEPAC Test	Oral Points	Report Points	Final Grade	Date
01											
02											
03											
04											
05											
06											
07											
08											
09											
10											

Spelling/Electives

LP#	Self Test Scores by Sections 1	2	3	4	5	Self Test Points	LIFEPAC Test	Oral Points	Report Points	Final Grade	Date
01											
02											
03											
04											
05											
06											
07											
08											
09											
10											

INSTRUCTIONS FOR BIBLE

The LIFEPAC curriculum from grades 2 through 12 is structured so that the daily instructional material is written directly into the LIFEPACs. The student is encouraged to read and follow this instructional material in order to develop independent study habits. The teacher should introduce the LIFEPAC to the student, set a required completion schedule, complete teacher checks, be available for questions regarding both content and procedures, administer and grade tests, and develop additional learning activities as desired. Teachers working with several students may schedule their time so that students are assigned to a quiet work activity when it is necessary to spend instructional time with one particular student.

The Teacher Notes section of the guide lists the required or suggested materials for the LIFEPACs and provides additional learning activities for the students. The materials section refers only to LIFEPAC materials and does not include materials which may be needed for the additional activities. Additional learning activities provide a change from the daily school routine, encourage the student's interest in learning and may be used as a reward for good study habits.

BIBLE 1001

Unit 1: Creation to Abraham

TEACHER NOTES

MATERIALS NEEDED FOR LIFEPAC	
Required	Suggested
• none	• Bible maps • Bible, King James Version • other versions of the Bible if permitted • Bible handbook • Bible atlas • the reference materials can be in either book or online formats

ADDITIONAL LEARNING ACTIVITIES

Section 1: Creation

1. Discuss these questions with your class.
   a. What is the difference between Creation and evolution?
   b. Was Jesus with God at the Creation of the earth?
   c. In 2 Peter 3:8 it says, "One day with the Lord is as a thousand years, and a thousand years as one day." Some have suggested from this verse that the "days" of Creation were 1,000 years in length. What do you think?
2. Arrange a visit to a Jewish synagogue and ask to look at a Hebrew Old Testament.
3. For a class project, draw a mural for your classroom illustrating the six (or seven) days of Creation.
4. At the beginning of this LIFEPAC, a number of quotations are given by famous people telling what the Bible meant to them. Write a brief statement summarizing what God's Word means to you.
5. Write a 100-word report on "Man's Place in a Christian Home." Then, write an additional 100 words on "Woman's Place in a Christian Home."

Section 2: Fall

1. Discuss these questions with your class.
   a. Why do you think Abel's offering was accepted when Cain's was rejected? (See Hebrews 11:4)
   b. Should parents blame themselves for their children's sin?
   c. Do we always recognize Satan when he comes to us? (Point out that he comes as an angel of light. Stress the fact that evil thoughts or negative thoughts come from him and that he creates doubt and suspicion in our minds.)

2. Select four members of the class for a panel discussion or divide into small groups to discuss the following question: Genesis 4:25 tells us that God gave Adam and Eve another son named Seth (which means substitute), and from his line came the chosen Hebrew nation and such men as Enoch and Noah. Do you think God forgave Adam and Eve for their sin and gave them a second chance?
3. Using a Bible map, find the approximate location of the Garden of Eden.
4. Using a Bible dictionary or concordance, list all the names you can find for Satan.
5. After Cain killed Abel he asked the question, "Am I my brother's keeper?" From a Christian viewpoint, write a 100-word essay on our responsibility to our neighbor today.
6. Prior to starting Section 3, begin writing a five-page report on the Flood. Use Scripture to support your viewpoint and include identification of the "sons of God," "daughters of men," and the "men of renown." Extra credit will be given to students who mention the variety of views regarding the cause of the Flood.

Section 3: Flood

1. Discuss these questions with your class.
   a. Why did Noah build the ark in the middle of the desert and try to describe rain to people who had never seen it before?
   b. What tensions could arise from eight people (including in-laws) living together for five months?
   c. What was it like being with all those animals (two of each plus those that multiplied during that time)?
   d. What was it like getting off the boat and being the only people on the face of the earth?
2. Have students locate Mt. Ararat on a Bible map.
3. Write and produce a skit about the Flood, showing people laughing at Noah, then later pounding on the door of the ark to get in after the rains came. This scene may be done in pantomime.
4. If God were to bring judgment to the world today, would you be one who would find "grace in the eyes of the Lord"?

Section 4: Nations

1. Discuss these questions with your class.
   a. Would you have expected Noah's descendants to have been more obedient to God after the Flood? Why were they so rebellious? (They still had a sinful nature.)
   b. If God promised that the world would never again be destroyed by a flood, why do we still have floods today?
2. Look up the word *antediluvian* in a dictionary. Write down the definition and the derivation of the word.
3. Make a genealogy chart showing the descendants of Noah, as shown in Genesis, Chapters 10 and 11.
4. Have a contest to see who can make the most words out of *antediluvian.*
5. If you lived during that time, would you have joined in the building of the Tower of Babel?

STUDENT WORKSHEETS

The activity on the following page may be reproduced as a student worksheet.

» ANSWER KEY

Any ten Messianic promises in the Old Testament will satisfy the requirements of this activity.

Administer the LIFEPAC Test.
The test is to be administered in one session. Give no help except with directions.
Evaluate the tests and review areas where the students have done poorly.
Review the pages and activities that stress the concepts tested.
If necessary, administer the Alternate LIFEPAC Test.

» THE PROMISE OF THE SAVIOR

You have learned that Genesis 3:15 is the first promise of the coming Messiah, our Savior, the Lord Jesus Christ. The Old Testament is full of other promises that Jesus will come. Using a topical Bible, Bible handbook, Bible dictionary, or Bible encyclopedia, find ten additional promises of the coming of the Messiah from ten different books of the Old Testament. Write the location and the entire verse on these lines. For additional credit, memorize some of the verses you find.

1. ______________________________
   ____
2. ______________________________
   ____
3. ______________________________
   ____
4. ______________________________
   ____
5. ______________________________
   ____
6. ______________________________
   ____
7. ______________________________
   ____
8. ______________________________
   ____
9. ______________________________
   ____
10. ______________________________
    ____

ANSWER KEYS

INTRODUCTION

I-1 true
I-2 true
I-3 true
I-4 true
I-5 true
I-6 true
I-7 true
I-8 true
I-9 true
I-10 true
I-11 false
I-12 true
I-13 God-breathed
I-14 Either order:
a. the Old Testament
b. the New Testament
I-15 sixty-six
I-16 thirty-nine
I-17 twenty-seven
I-18 Pentateuch
I-19 a. Genesis
b. Exodus
c. Leviticus
d. Numbers
e. Deuteronomy

SECTION 1

1.1 Genesis
1.2 eleven
1.3 a. create
b. bring into existence
c. make
d. nothing
1.4 Creation
1.5 a. light
b. firmament
c. seas and dry land
d. sun, moon, and stars
e. lower animal life (fish and fowl)
f. higher animal life (beast) and man
1.6 The plural personal pronoun "us" refers to all the members of the Godhead—the Father, the Son, and the Holy Spirit.
1.7 moral and spiritual nature
1.8 to have dominion over it
1.9 to fill
1.10 one woman for one man

SELF TEST 1

1.01 c
1.02 b
1.03 c
1.04 a
1.05 d
1.06 revelation
1.07 redemption
1.08 inspiration
1.09 a. fourteen
b. forty
1.010 salvation
1.011 a. Old Testament
b. New Testament
1.012 introduction
1.013 Pentateuch
1.014 e
1.015 f
1.016 b
1.017 a
1.018 g
1.019 d
1.020 true
1.021 true
1.022 true
1.023 false
1.024 true
1.025 false
1.026 false
1.027 true
1.028 true
1.029 Example:
The plural personal pronoun "us" is used to identify all the members of the Godhead—the Father, the Son, and the Holy Spirit.
1.030 Example:
For man to be made in the image of God evidently means to be made with a moral and spiritual nature.

SECTION 2

2.1 sin
2.2 Any order:
a. serpent
b. dragon
c. Devil
2.3 true
2.4 false
2.5 b
2.6 a. Christ
b. Satan
2.7 Either order:
a. sin against righteousness
b. the devil against God
2.8 Genesis 3:15
2.9 Satan
2.10 true
2.11 death
2.12 a. rejected
b. accepted
2.13 a. substitute
b. Seth
2.14 a. Hebrew
b. promised seed or Messiah
2.15 Either order:
a. Enoch
b. Noah

SELF TEST 2

2.01 true
2.02 false
2.03 false
2.04 true
2.05 false
2.06 true
2.07 true
2.08 true
2.09 true
2.010 false
2.011 c
2.012 b
2.013 a
2.014 c
2.015 d
2.016 Seth
2.017 a. Abel
b. Cain
c. promised seed or Messiah
2.018 one
2.019 canon
2.020 generations
2.021 Pentateuch
2.022 Creation
2.023 to fill
2.024 b
2.025 e
2.026 a
2.027 f *or* d
2.028 c
2.029 Answers will vary, but should include the following ideas: The fruit appealed to (1) the lust of the flesh: was good for food; (2) the lust of the eyes: was pleasant to look upon; and (3) the pride of life: would make one wise.
2.030 Answers will vary, but should include the following ideas:
the immediate result was spiritual death;
the ultimate result was physical death.

SECTION 3

3.1 Noah
3.2 a. eight
b. ark
3.3 a. Noah
b. wife
c. sons
d. wives
3.4 a. five
b. Mount Ararat
3.5 a. an altar
b. burnt offerings or sacrifices
3.6 rainbow
3.7 destroy the earth with a flood
3.8 a. Shem
b. Ham
c. Japheth
3.9 Any order:
a. other inspired biblical writers
b. the Lord Jesus Himself
c. tradition
d. archaeology
3.10 traditions
3.11 archaeology
3.12 c
3.13 b
3.14 a

SELF TEST 3

3.01 a
3.02 c
3.03 b
3.04 e
3.05 c
3.06 a. eight
b. ark
3.07 Any order:
a. Noah
b. Noah's wife
c. Noah's sons
d. Noah's sons' wives
3.08 Any order:
a. Shem
b. Ham
c. Japheth
3.09 substitute
3.010 false
3.011 false
3.012 true
3.013 true
3.014 true

SECTION 4

4.1 a. spoke
b. language
4.2 did not fulfill
4.3 sinful (rebellious)
4.4 gate of God
4.5 confusion
4.6 ziggurat
4.7 Example:
They determined to prevent any future destruction from a flood by building a tower (a terraced building) that would reach into heaven.
4.8 a. confused their language
b. caused their dispersion
4.9 a. Asia
b. Africa
c. Asia Minor and Europe

SELF TEST 4

4.01 false
4.02 false
4.03 true
4.04 false
4.05 true
4.06 true
4.07 true
4.08 true
4.09 false
4.010 false
4.011 d
4.012 h
4.013 b
4.014 g
4.015 a
4.016 e
4.017 j *or* k
4.018 1
4.019 f
4.020 c
4.021 Example:
Rejecting God's promise to Noah and the sign of that promise, men at Babel probably determined to prevent any future destruction from a flood by building a tower (a terraced building) that would reach into heaven.
4.022 For man to be made in the image of God evidently means to be made with a moral and spiritual nature.

LIFEPAC TEST

1. b
2. d
3. d
4. a
5. b
6. true
7. false
8. true
9. false
10. false
11. Either order:
a. moral
b. spiritual
12. a. Old Testament
b. New Testament
13. spiritual
14. Example:
They determined to prevent any future destruction from a flood by building a tower (a terraced building) that would reach into heaven.
15. Any order:
a. other-inspired biblical writers
b. the Lord Jesus Himself
c. tradition
d. archaeology
16. g
17. f
18. b
19. d
20. e

ALTERNATE LIFEPAC TEST

1. c
2. f
3. d
4. b
5. a
6. j
7. h
8. k
9. i
10. g
11. false
12. true
13. true
14. false
15. true
16. true
17. true
18. true
19. true
20. true
21. 1300 B.C.
22. a. five
b. scroll or book(s)
23. substitute
24. Ararat
25. sin
26. God
27. revelation
28. Satan
29. Savior
30. rainbow
31. c
32. a
33. b
34. c
35. b
36. a. Law
b. History
c. Poetry
d. Major Prophets
e. Minor Prophets
37. Any order:
a. Shem
b. Ham
c. Japheth
38. a. Genesis
b. Exodus
c. Leviticus
d. Numbers
e. Deuteronomy

BIBLE 1001

ALTERNATE LIFEPAC TEST

NAME ________________________

DATE ________________________

SCORE ________________________

Match these items (each answer, 2 points).

1.	________ antediluvian	a.	in the beginning
2.	________ Elohim	b.	father of the Hebrews
3.	________ toledhoth	c.	period before the Flood
4.	________ Eber	d.	generations
5.	________ Bereshith	e.	Noah
6.	________ Cain	f.	God
7.	________ ziggurat	g.	shrewd
8.	________ fiat	h.	tower
9.	________ bara	i.	to create from nothing
10.	________ subtle	j.	a murderer
		k.	an order or command

Write true or false (each answer, 1 point).

11. ____________ The word *canon* refers to the first five books of the Old Testament.

12. ____________ Josephus was a Jewish historian.

13. ____________ Cain was a farmer and Abel was a shepherd.

14. ____________ The name of Adam and Eve's third son was Shem.

15. ____________ A ziggurat was built in Babel.

16. ____________ The Pentateuch is also called the books of the Law.

17. ____________ The book of Genesis contains fifty chapters.

18. ____________ The Old Testament contains thirty-nine books.

19. ____________ Ham and Japheth were brothers.

20. ____________ *Bab-El* means *the gate of God.*

Complete these statements (each answer, 3 points).

21. The earliest writing of any part of the Bible was about ____________________ .

22. The word *Pentateuch* comes from two Greek words meaning a. ____________________ and b. ____________________ .

23. The word *Seth* means ____________________ .

24. The ark came to rest upon Mt. ____________________ .

25. Like antediluvian men, Noah's descendants were men with ____________________ natures.

26. The author of the Bible is ____________________ .

27. The Bible is God's ____________________ of Himself to man.

28. The serpent who tempted the woman in the garden was ____________________ .

29. Genesis 3:15 is the first promise of the coming ____________________ .

30. The sign of the covenant God made with Noah was the ____________________ .

Write the letter for the correct answer on each line (each answer, 2 points).

31. The Bible was written over a period of ________ years.
a. 1200 b. 1300 c. 1400 d. 1500

32. On the fourth day of Creation, God created ________ .
a. the sun, moon, and stars b. fish
c. the seas d. man

33. The Hebrew word *ish* means ________ .
a. woman b. man c. Eve d. God

34. When the Flood came upon the earth, only ________ people survived.
a. ten b. eleven c. eight d. none of these

35. The two foes mentioned in Genesis 3:15 are ________ .
a. Adam and Eve b. Christ and Satan c. Cain and Abel d. sin and evil

Complete these activities (each answer, 3 points).

36. List in order the five divisions of the English Old Testament.

a. ______________________ b. ______________________

c. ______________________ d. ______________________

e. ______________________

37. List the three sons of Noah.

a. ______________ b. ______________ c. ______________

38. List in order the five books of the Pentateuch.

a. ______________________ b. ______________________

c. ______________________ d. ______________________

e. ______________________

BIBLE 1002

Unit 2: Abraham to Moses

TEACHER NOTES

MATERIALS NEEDED FOR LIFEPAC	
Required	Suggested
• none	• Bible, King James Version • other versions of the Bible if permitted • Bible handbook • paperback atlas of Bible lands • the reference materials can be in either book or online formats

ADDITIONAL LEARNING ACTIVITIES

Section 1: Abraham

1. Christ said in the New Testament that it was harder for a rich man to enter heaven than for a camel to go through the eye of a needle. Compare Abraham with the rich young ruler in Luke chapter 18.
2. Abraham is known as a man of faith, but do you think he showed faith when he introduced Sarah as his sister because he feared the Egyptians would kill him and take her?
3. Go to the school or city library or use their website. Using the *Readers' Guide* or an online periodical database such as EBSCOHost, locate some magazine articles on archaeological discoveries from the days of Abraham. Several students together should prepare summaries of these articles.
4. God's call to Abraham included both a promise and a command. Can you think of a time in your life when God asked you to do something you thought was hard, but He made it easier? Share this experience in writing with your teacher.

Section 2: Isaac

1. Are you willing to follow Christ, as did Abraham, even though you do not know where He may lead? Share your answer in writing.
2. Discuss the importance of finding the right mate and letting God lead in this part of our lives.
3. Read Genesis chapter 24. Write and perform a skit depicting Isaac's and Rebekah's courtship and marriage.
4. Man's weaknesses and strengths are both presented in Scripture. Make a list of what you believe are your strong points and a second list of your weaknesses. Leave room next to the second column to write Scripture verses that will help you to overcome your weaknesses.

Section 3: Jacob

1. Review the personalities of Jacob and Esau and discuss how children born to the same parents often turn out to be different.
2. When Esau sold his birthright to Jacob and Jacob tricked his father into giving him the blessing, was Jacob the only one guilty or should his mother, Rebekah, have also shared the blame?
3. Have a group make a list of the high points of Jacob's life and see how God was leading him. Then have students make a list of high points in their lives and share how the Lord has led them.
4. Perform skits depicting Esau selling his birthright and Jacob receiving blind Isaac's blessing.
5. Write a 100-word report of how Rebekah suffered for aiding Jacob in his deceiving Isaac.
6. After completing Section 3 students may write a 200-word report dealing with the question of whether parents should be responsible for the sins of their children. The report should use Jacob as an illustration.

Section 4: Joseph

1. Discuss Jacob's loving Joseph more than the others, and the jealousy it created. Does this kind of thing happen today?
2. Should a Christian be jealous of someone who has more "talents"? (It should make them work harder on their own capabilities.)
3. Why do you think Joseph was not bitter against his brothers and against God?
4. Act out the story of Joseph up to the time he was sold as a slave.
5. Write an outline of the life of Joseph.
6. Do you know someone today who, like Joseph, has gone through many problems that, instead of making them bitter, has brought them closer to God? You may want to call or write them this week, letting them know how much you appreciate them.
7. Have the student read the story of Joseph after he was sold into slavery and notice the number of times the phrase, "...and the Lord was with Joseph," is used.

STUDENT WORKSHEETS

The activity on the following page may be reproduced as a student worksheet.

» ANSWER KEY

Any reasonable answer is acceptable.

Administer the LIFEPAC Test.
The test is to be administered in one session. Give no help except with directions.
Evaluate the tests and review areas where the students have done poorly.
Review the pages and activities that stress the concepts tested.
If necessary, administer the Alternate LIFEPAC Test.

» THE BOOK OF GENESIS

In Bible LIFEPAC 1002 you have studied the revelation of God's plan from Abraham to the sojourn in Egypt. Information concerning this period of divine history is recorded in Genesis chapters 12–50. Quickly read each chapter and make up a title for that chapter. The title should mean something to you. Put it in your own words. Write the titles on these lines and memorize them during this school year.

Genesis 12 ______________________

Genesis 13 ______________________

Genesis 14 ______________________

Genesis 15 ______________________

Genesis 16 ______________________

Genesis 17 ______________________

Genesis 18 ______________________

Genesis 19 ______________________

Genesis 20 ______________________

Genesis 21 ______________________

Genesis 22 ______________________

Genesis 23 ______________________

Genesis 24 ______________________

Genesis 25 ______________________

Genesis 26 ______________________

Genesis 27 ______________________

Genesis 28 ______________________

Genesis 29 ______________________

Genesis 30 ______________________

Genesis 31 ______________________

Genesis 32 ______________________

Genesis 33 ______________________

Genesis 34 ______________________

Genesis 35 ______________________

Genesis 36 ______________________

Genesis 37 ______________________

Genesis 38 ______________________

Genesis 39 ______________________

Genesis 40 ______________________

Genesis 41 ______________________

Genesis 42 ______________________

Genesis 43 ______________________

Genesis 44 ______________________

Genesis 45 ______________________

Genesis 46 ______________________

Genesis 47 ______________________

Genesis 48 ______________________

Genesis 49 ______________________

Genesis 50 ______________________

ANSWER KEYS

SECTION 1

1.1 biographies
1.2 ruling father
1.3 Abraham
1.4 a. main events
b. outstanding individuals
1.5 a. Ur
b. Chaldees
1.6 Shem
1.7 Abram
1.8 Terah
1.9 Either order:
a. Nahor
b. Haran
1.10 Lot
1.11 a. cuneiform tablets
b. Nebuchadnezzar's temples
1.12 Any order:
a. flocks
b. gold
c. servants or herds, silver
1.13 2000 B.C.
1.14 Babylonia
1.15 a. Abraham
b. father of a great multitude
1.16 a. Sarah
b. princess
1.17 a. Terah
b. Lot
1.18 Haran
1.19 Haran
1.20 a. Stephen or Stephen's address
b. Acts 7:2-4
1.21 Either order:
a. a command
b. a promise
1.22 Savior
1.23 built an altar
1.24 Egypt
1.25 He lied about his wife.
1.26 a. provision
b. protection
1.27 Take her and go thy way.
1.28 all his possessions
1.29 a. Bethel
b. the altar he had made there
1.30 nothing
1.31 all
1.32 covetous
1.33 a. son
b. stars
1.34 righteousness
1.35 a. circumcision
b Isaac

SELF TEST 1

1.01 f
1.02 d
1.03 a
1.04 e
1.05 b
1.06 ruling father
1.07 wealth
1.08 Haran
1.09 Ur of the Chaldees
1.010 Savior
1.011 Nahor
1.012 into a land that He would show him
1.013 a great nation of Abraham's descendants
1.014 faith
1.015 innumerable as the stars
1.016 true
1.017 true
1.018 false
1.019 false
1.020 true
1.021 c
1.022 c
1.023 c
1.024 a
1.025 d

SECTION 2

2.1 laughter
2.2 a. 100
b. 90
2.3 named
2.4 to raise up
2.5 to prove or tempt (the faith of)
2.6 find Isaac a wife
2.7 a. Rebekah
b. Bethuel
c. Nahor
2.8 Laban
2.9 a. Jacob
b. Esau
2.10 a. Abraham
b. Isaac
2.11 26:1-5

SELF TEST 2

2.01 true
2.02 true
2.03 false
2.04 false
2.05 true
2.06 a
2.07 c
2.08 b
2.09 b
2.010 d
2.011 a. Isaac
b. Christ
2.012 a. Abraham
b. Isaac
2.013 a. Abraham
b. Isaac
2.014 Bethuel
2.015 provide the world a Savior
2.016 a. father Terah
b. brother Nahor
2.017 e
2.018 a
2.019 f
2.020 b
2.021 c

SECTION 3

3.1 20
3.2 a. nations
b. stronger
3.3 a. elder
b. younger
3.4 a. Esau
b. Jacob
3.5 false
3.6 a. birthright
b. eat
3.7 a. her homeland or Haran
b. to be protected from Esau
3.8 a. Bethel
b. dream
3.9 a. Abraham
b. Isaac
3.10 a. a vow or compact
b. Genesis 28:20-22
3.11 a. family
b. kindred
3.12 a. Bethuel
b. Nahor
3.13 Either order:
a. Leah
b. Rachel
3.14 eleven
3.15 a. twenty
b. fourteen
3.16 a. trickery
b. deceit or deception
3.17 Israel, a prince with God
3.18 a. Esau
b. peace
3.19 Shechem
3.20 land
3.21 a. twelfth or youngest
b. Rachel
3.22 a. Rachel
b. Hebron
3.23 a. Joseph
b. kill
3.24 a. Joseph
b. Reuben
3.25 a. Joseph
b. Egypt
3.26 a. mourned
b. dead

SELF TEST 3

3.01 b
3.02 c
3.03 a
3.04 d
3.05 a
3.06 true
3.07 true
3.08 true
3.09 false
3.010 true
3.011 d
3.012 f
3.013 a
3.014 b
3.015 a
3.016 throw him in a pit
3.017 a. Jacob
b. Joseph
3.018 Either order:
a. Jacob
b. Laban
3.019 Either order:
a. Leah
b. Rachel
3.020 Rachel
3.021 a. Midianite merchantmen
b. Egypt

SECTION 4

4.1 Either order:
a. Joseph
b. Benjamin
4.2 Benjamin
4.3 Example:
of the death of his mother, Rachel, whom Jacob loved so much
4.4 a. jealousy
b. hate
4.5 dreams
4.6 pit
4.7 Joseph was dead or had been slain by a wild beast
4 8 a. Potiphar
b. Pharaoh
4.9 a. that the Lord was with him
b. that the Lord made all that He did to prosper
4.10 of the false accusation of Potiphar's wife
4.11 true
4.12 Either order (a, b):
a. butler
b. baker
c. Pharaoh himself
4.13 faithful
4.14 a. humiliation
b. exaltation
4.15 30
4.16 God
4.17 wise course of action
4.18 a. seven
b. seven
4.19 Egypt
4.20 Either order:
a. Egypt
b. Joseph
4.21 a. built an altar and worshiped God with a sacrifice
b. gave Jacob assurance that He would bring them out of Egypt
4.22 a. instruction
b. blessing
4.23 Goshen
4.24 a. Judah
b. Genesis 49:10
4.25 Reuben
4.26 forty-eight
4.27 Either order:
a. Ephraim
b. Manasseh

4.28 Either order:
a. Joseph
b. Levi
4.29 110
4.30 delivered Israel from Egyptian bondage

SELF TEST 4

4.01 false
4.02 true
4.03 true
4.04 true
4.05 false
4.06 b
4.07 c
4.08 d
4.09 a
4.010 a
4.011 a. plenty
b. famine
4.012 Chaldea
4.013 the Lord
4.014 butler
4.015 to provide the world a Savior
4.016 Example:
Abraham counted upon the fact that God was able to raise up Isaac, even from the dead.
4.017 Any order:
a. Two nations were in her womb.
b. One people would be stronger than the other.
c. The older would serve the younger.
4.018 It was because of the death of his mother, Rachel, whom Jacob loved so much.
4.019 The message was that Israel's Messiah, the Savior of the world, would come through the tribe of Judah.
4.020 b
4.021 f
4.022 a
4.023 e
4.024 c

LIFEPAC TEST

1. e
2. f
3. b
4. a
5. c
6. false
7. true
8. false
9. true
10. false
11. c
12. b
13. c
14. d
15. a
16. 2000
17. a. 100
    b. 90
18. a. permanent
    b. immediate
19. Example:
    the special object of his father's love and favor
20. a. to spare Joseph's life
    b. to deliver him later from the pit
21. Either order:
    a. Ephraim
    b. Manasseh

ALTERNATE LIFEPAC TEST

1. true
2. false
3. true
4. false
5. false
6. d
7. a
8. e
9. f
10. b
11. b
12. c
13. a
14. c
15. b
16. Egypt
17. Terah
18. a. spiritual
    b. material
19. Bethel
20. a. 100
    b. 90
21. Any order:
    a. Haran
    b. Sheehem
    c. Bethel
    d. Egypt
22. Either order:
    a. Jacob
    b. Esau
23. Either order:
    a. Rachel
    b. Leah
24. Either order:
    a. Ephraim
    b. Manasseh

BIBLE 1002

ALTERNATE LIFEPAC TEST

NAME ______________________

DATE ______________________

SCORE ______________________

Answer true or false (each answer, 1 point).

1. ____________ Sarah was Abraham's half-sister.
2. ____________ When Abraham and Lot separated, Abraham took his family to the city of Sodom.
3. ____________ Abraham's servant found a wife for Isaac in the city of Nahor.
4. ____________ Jacob was older than Esau.
5. ____________ Joseph was the son of Jacob and Leah.

Match these items (each answer, 2 points).

6. ________ Ur of the Chaldees
7. ________ Sodom
8. ________ Peniel
9. ________ Ephrath
10. ________ Egypt

a. Lot
b. Joseph
c. Ezekiel
d. Abraham
e. Jacob
f. Benjamin

Write the letter for the correct answer on each line (each answer, 2 points).

11. A patriarch was a ________ .
a. pharaoh b. ruling father c. king d. ruler

12. Historians place Abraham at around the year ________ B.C.
a. 1800 b. 1900 c. 2000 d. 2100

13. The name *Isaac* means ________ .
a. laughter b. miracle of God c. born in old age d. contentious

14. Jacob worked ________ years for Rachel.
a. 7 b. 10 c. 14 d. 21

15. Joseph was ________ years old when he became ruler of Egypt.
a. 25 b. 30 c. 32 d. 35

Complete these sentences (each answer, 3 points).

16. Abraham's response to the famine in Canaan was a journey to ____________ .

17. Abraham's father's name was ____________ .

18. Jacob appreciated a. ____________ values, but Esau was concerned more with b. ____________ affairs.

19. Jacob had a vision of a ladder at ____________ .

20. When Isaac was promised, Abraham was a. ____________ years old, and Sarah was b. ____________ years old.

Complete these activities (each answer, 3 points).

21. List four places visited by Abraham.

a. ________________________ b. ________________________

c. ________________________ d. ________________________

22. Name Isaac's two sons.

a. ________________________ b. ________________________

23. Name Jacob's wives.

a. ________________________ b. ________________________

24. Name Joseph's two sons.

a. ________________________ b. ________________________

BIBLE 1003

Unit 3: Exodus and Wanderings

TEACHER NOTES

MATERIALS NEEDED FOR LIFEPAC	
Required	Suggested
• none	• Bible, King James Version • other versions of the Bible if permitted • Bible atlas • maps of the Bible lands during the time of the Exodus • concordance • thesaurus • the reference materials can be in either book or online formats

ADDITIONAL LEARNING ACTIVITIES

Section 1: Exodus

1. Set the classroom up as a map of Egypt and Sinai and have the students "walk through" the events of the early period of the Exodus.
2. Discuss the parallels between the bondage of the Israelites in Egypt and the bondage of Christians today in foreign lands. This discussion may also deal with questions concerning slavery.
3. Have a small group of students discuss the release of the Hebrews from Egypt. Have one group take the Egyptian view and another group the Israelite view.
4. Have a group of students compose a time line and a map that would show the events of the Hebrews during the early portion of the wilderness wanderings.
5. Read the Ten Commandments as listed in Exodus chapter 20. With the use of a concordance, find any references to these laws in the New Testament. You may even find where the New Testament writers quote certain commandments.
6. Using a concordance, find all the Biblical references to Moses that occur outside the first five books of the Bible.

Section 2: Leviticus

1. Discuss the relationship and typology of the feasts and sacrifices to the Lord Jesus Christ. Many good books deal with this subject and are readily available for reference material.
2. Visit a Jewish synagogue with the class and note the various structures that have been included in the synagogue that reflect the Levitical order.
3. Have a group of students put on a short play that will portray the activities and events of the Day of Atonement.

4. Have a group of students make a model of the Tabernacle, with both exterior and interior details.
5. Make a calendar that gives the dates of all the feasts and holy days of the Jewish year. This calendar may be made into a poster and displayed in the classroom when completed.
6. Using either the Passover or the Day of Atonement, compare the traditional events and activities of these times with the modern Jewish observation of these days. List those things included and those things that have been excluded from the observance.

Section 3: Numbers

1. Have the classroom set up as the Sinai, and with the students, "walk through" the latter period of the wilderness wanderings.
2. Divide the group into two sections and debate or discuss the report of the spies as they returned from the land of Canaan. One group should argue for an immediate journey to the land. The other should favor waiting (Reference–Numbers 13).
3. Allow a group of students to make a large poster for display that shows the organization of the tribes of Israel around the Tabernacle.
4. Using the census recorded in Numbers chapters 1 and 26, mathematically tally up the number of people involved in the wilderness wanderings. Find a total and also the individual number according to each tribe.
5. Compose chapter titles in your own words for each of the chapters of the book of Numbers. Make sure the titles are relevant to the subject matter.
6. Following completion of Section 3, the student may write a four-page report that deals with the error or sin of complaining. As the Hebrews murmured while in the wilderness, believers do today. The student should integrate into the report the principle of promises from the Lord and New Testament passages that prohibit complaining. Emphasis should be placed upon the faithfulness of God.

Section 4: Deuteronomy

1. Discuss who might have written the closing portion of the book of Deuteronomy, which relates the death of Moses. Was it written by Moses prior to his death? Could Joshua have written it? Point out that no definite answer has been found.
2. Discuss the reasons Moses left out the history of the wilderness wanderings in the review of Israel's journey recorded in Deuteronomy chapters 1–4. See Section 4 of this LIFEPAC for resource information.
3. Have a group of students make a chart or poster that compares Deuteronomy, the second law, with the book of Exodus and the original revelation of the law. Numerous parallel passages may be found.
4. Divide a group of students into two sections and debate or discuss whether the prophecies of Deuteronomy have been fulfilled and if not, if they ever will be.
5. Using a concordance or a topical Bible, make a list of the New Testament books that quote verses, either fully or in part, from Deuteronomy.
6. Using a thesaurus, find as many synonyms and antonyms for the word *law* as possible. Check those that can refer to the law of God.

STUDENT WORKSHEET

The activity on the following page may be reproduced as a student worksheet.

» ANSWER KEY

IN PHARAOH'S HOUSE

1520 B.C.	1480 B.C.
	Birth

ON THE BACK SIDE OF THE DESERT

1480 B.C.	1440 B.C.
	The Exodus

IN THE WILDERNESS

1440 B.C.	1400 B.C.
	Death

Administer the LIFEPAC Test.
The test is to be administered in one session. Give no help except with directions.
Evaluate the tests and review areas where the students have done poorly.
Review the pages and activities that stress the concepts tested.
If necessary, administer the Alternate LIFEPAC Test.

» THE LIFE OF MOSES

The life of Moses can easily be divided into three sections of forty years each as shown. Using a Bible handbook, Bible dictionary, or Bible encyclopedia, assign approximate dates to the following time line. On the time line indicate when important events in the life of Moses occurred. After you complete this project, you may wish to reproduce it on a larger scale and display it in the classroom.

IN PHARAOH'S HOUSE

_______________ B.C. _______________ B.C.

____

Birth

ON THE BACK SIDE OF THE DESERT

_______________ B.C. _______________ B.C.

____

The Exodus

IN THE WILDERNESS

_______________ B.C. _______________ B.C.

____

Death

ANSWER KEYS

SECTION 1

1.1 1570
1.2 a. Semites
b. 1730
1.3 Ahmose
1.4 Either order:
a. Joseph
b. Israel
1.5 Ahmose
1.6 Either order:
a. number
b. power
1.7 Either order:
a. multiply faster
b. grow stronger
1.8 failed
1.9 feared
1.10 great nation
1.11 a. Amram
b. Jochebed
1.12 a. Miriam
b. Aaron
1.13 Pharaoh's daughter
1.14 Levi
1.15 "to draw out of the water"
1.16 a. forty
b. Midian
1.17 a. enjoy the pleasures of sin for a season
b. the treasures in Egypt
1.18 Example:
He turned Pharaoh's wicked scheme into the very means of raising up a deliverer and preparing a deliverance for His people, which Pharaoh had feared.
1.19 Example:
He chose to identify himself with his people, the people of God, and to follow God's plan for his life.
1.20 forty
1.21 a. Jethro
b. Zipporah
1.22 Either order:
a. Gershom
b. Eliezer
1.23 a. a burning bush
b. the mountain of God (or Horeb or Sinai)
1.24 eighty
1.25 a. anger of God
b. a helper
c. Aaron
1.26 Any order:
a. that God is holy and must be approached with reverence and awe
b. that the God Who spoke to him was the God of his father, of Abraham, of Isaac, and of Jacob
c. that God had seen the affliction of His people and had heard their prayers
d. that God would deliver His people from Egypt and to the Promised Land
1.27 a. Who am I?
b. Certainly I will be with thee.
c. What shall I say to them?
d. I AM hath sent me unto you.
e. They will not believe me.
f. What is that in thine hand?
g. I am not eloquent.
h. I will teach thee what thou shalt say.
1.28 Any order:
a. changing his rod to a serpent and back to his rod
b. making his hand leprous and whole again
c. changing water to blood
1.29 Aaron
1.30 a. negative
b. increase
c. workload
1.31 deliver Israel from Egypt to Canaan
1.32 Who is the LORD, that I should obey his voice to let Israel go?
1.33 show His superior power and provision for His people
1.34 Either order:
a. His power
b. the powerlessness of Egyptian idols
1.35 the last seven more severe plagues did not occur in Goshen where the Israelites lived
1.36 a. death
b. blood
c. lamb
1.37 God's redemptive plan for lost man
1.38 God's plan for the Passover
1.39 obedience to His commands
1.40 death angel entered and slew the firstborn
1.41 a. a pillar of cloud
b. a pillar of fire
1.42 Red Sea
1.43 Migdol
1.44 He was God

1.45 Fear ye not, stand still and see the salvation of the LORD, which he will show to you today.
1.46 a. light
b. darkness
1.47 the Lord was fighting for Israel against Egypt
1.48 they were in the Promised Land
1.49 Any order:
a. Marah
b. Elim
c. Wilderness of Sin
d. Rephidim
1.50 a. Rephidim
b. Amalekites
c. destroy
d. write
e. book
1.51 a. water
b. Marah
c. sweet
1.52 a. the Wilderness of Sin
b. meat or quail
c. manna
d. obedience
1.53 a. Sabbath
b. the Wilderness (of Sin)
1.54 a. water
b. seventy
c. Elim
1.55 a. a rock
b. Christ
1.56 a. Sinai
b. three
1.57 Teacher
1.58 a. Exodus
b. Leviticus
c. Numbers
1.59 Any order:
a. the Law
b. the Tabernacle
c. the Priesthood
1.60 true
1.61 a. outline *or* a. spoken
b. detail b. written
1.62 Either order:
a. moral
b. ceremonial
1.63 a. moral law
b. ceremonial law
1.64 a. holiness
b. sinfulness
c. need of a Savior
1.65 Christ (His redemptive work)
1.66 type of Jesus Christ
1.67 (the living) God
1.68 d
1.69 f
1.70 c
1.71 g
1.72 a
1.73 h
1.74 b
1.75 Priesthood
1.76 Christ
1.77 a. Israel
b. Church
1.78 a. garments
b. priests
1.79 a. believer
b. Christ

SELF TEST 1

1.01 false
1.02 false
1.03 true
1.04 true
1.05 a
1.06 d
1.07 b
1.08 d
1.09 a
1.010 c
1.011 g
1.012 a
1.013 h
1.014 b
1.015 f
1.016 c
1.017 e
1.018 Any order:
a. changing his rod to a serpent and back to a rod
b. making his hand leprous and whole again
c. changing water to blood
1.019 a. Egypt or slavery
b. Canaan or the Promised Land
1.020 (moral) law
1.021 ceremonial (law)
1.022 He was God

SECTION 2

2.1 (the law of) offerings
2.2 a. burnt
b. meal
c. peace
d. sin
e. trespass
2.3 did not
2.4 The person and work of the Lord Jesus Christ
2.5 burnt
2.6 peace
2.7 trespass
2.8 burnt
2.9 sin
2.10 meal
2.11 priests
2.12 God's Word
2.13 blood
2.14 Jesus Christ
2.15 Any order:
a. Washed, Lev. 8:6 (Matthew 3:13-15)
b. Anointed, Lev. 8:12 (Matthew 3:16)
c. Offered, Lev. 8:14-29 (Hebrews 9:11-12)
d. Accepted, Lev. 9:24 (Matthew 3:17)
2.16 holy
2.17 sin
2.18 Either order (a, b):
a. cleansing
b. judgment
c. both
2.19 God
2.20 Any order:
a. offerings
b. priests
c. sin
2.21 a. recurs
b. detail or emphasis, clarification, amplification
2.22 Any order:
a. a day toward which all looked eagerly
b. a day when they would give themselves fully to penitence and humiliation
c. a day when the priest would go into the Most Holy Place and make atonement for all their sins
d. a day that pointed directly to Calvary and the whole redemptive work of Christ
2.23 Chapter 16
2.24 the door of the Tabernacle
2.25 blood
2.26 a. Who
b. what

2.27 Either order:
a. Egyptians
b. Canaanites

2.28 Either order:
a. people
b. priests

2.29 Any order:
a. Passover—redemption
b. Unleavened Bread—redemption
c. Firstfruits—Resurrection of Christ
d. Pentecost—coming of Holy Spirit, gathering of Church
e. Trumpets—awakening of Israel
f. Day of Atonement—Israel's repentance and restoration; acceptance of Messiah
g. Tabernacles—millennial restoration and rest

2.30 Any order:
a. the lamps and how they were to be kept
b. the oil by which the lamps were to be replenished
c. the table of shewbread, how the loaves were to be made, exchanged, and consumed

2.31 a. land
b. seventh

2.32 fiftieth

2.33 Either order:
a. joys
b. blessings

2.34 Any order:
a. Slaves were freed.
b. Debts were forgiven.
c. Exiles were returned home.
d. The poor had their possessions restored.

SELF TEST 2

2.01 a. burnt
b. meal
c. peace
d. sin
e. trespass

2.02 the person and work of the Lord Jesus Christ
2.03 God's plan for the Passover
2.04 1730
2.05 true
2.06 false
2.07 false
2.08 true
2.09 d
2.010 a
2.011 d
2.012 c
2.013 b
2.014 a
2.015 c
2.016 c
2.017 a
2.018 e
2.019 b
2.020 d
2.021 f

SECTION 3

3.1 three-part
3.2 twelve
3.3 Levi
3.4 a. Joseph
b. Ephraim
c. Manasseh
3.5 a. Levi
b. religious or priestly
3.6 Tabernacle
3.7 the presence of the Lord in their midst
3.8 jealously
3.9 taking the vow of a Nazarite
3.10 a. miraculous cloud or fire at night
b. Tabernacle
3.11 murmuring
3.12 Taberah
3.13 mixed multitude
3.14 manna
3.15 meat
3.16 a. judged or disciplined
b. murmuring
3.17 a. Kibroth-Hattaavah
b. the graves of lust
3.18 Hazeroth
3.19 murmured against Moses
3.20 Either order:
a. Joshua
b. Caleb
3.21 die in the wilderness
3.22 a. ignorance
b. presumptuous
3.23 presumptuous sin
3.24 a. Korah
b. Levite
3.25 Example:
God's judgment on Korah and his followers
3.26 the budding, blooming, and bearing fruit of Aaron's rod (yielding almonds)
3.27 struck the rock
3.28 a. unbelief
b. rebellion
3.29 to allow them to lead His people into the land of promise
3 30 a. Mount Hor
b. Eleazer
3.31 serpents
3.32 Christ
3.33 Moab
3.34 curse
3.35 Either order:
a. immorality
b. idolatry
3.36 a. a census of the new generation
b. the naming of Moses' successor
c. laws concerning worship, vows, and war
d a summary of Israel's journey from Egypt to Moab
e. instructions concerning the land of Canaan

SELF TEST 3

3.01 d
3.02 b
3.03 c
3.04 b
3.05 a
3.06 true
3.07 false
3.08 true
3.09 false
3.010 true
3.011 a. speak to
b. struck
3.012 die in the wilderness
3.013 (high) priest
3.014 c
3.015 e
3.016 b
3.017 d
3.018 f
3.019 Either order:
a. unbelief
b. rebellion
3.020 Nazarite
3.021 graves of lust
3.022 a. death
b. serpents

SECTION 4

4.1 a. Kadesh
b. Kadesh
c. Moab
4.2 wilderness wanderings
4.3 obedience
4.4 Ten Commandments
4.5 a. exposition
b. Commandments
4.6 Either order:
a. first
b. second
4.7 obedience
4.8 Law of God
4.9 a. blessings
b. obedience
4.10 a. curses
b. disobedience
4.11 a. curses
b. prophetic
4.12 a. 30:1-3
b. regathering
c. land
4.13 inspiration
4.14 a. go before them
b. go with them
4.15 Either order:
a. to read the Law to all Israel every seven years (at the Feast of Tabernacles)
b. to place the book of the Law, which Moses had written, into the Ark of the Covenant
4.16 a. write
b. teach to the children of Israel
4.17 a. Canaan (Promise)
b. Mount Nebo
4.18 Moab
4.19 Moses

SELF TEST 4

4.01 a. Sinai
b. Moab
4.02 5:4-22
4.03 6-26
4.04 a. Gerizim
b. blessings
4.05 a. Ebal
b. curses
4.06 Lord
4.07 Joshua
4.08 fulfilled prophecy
4.09 32:1-43
4.010 30:1-3
4.011 a. regather them
b. land
4.012 Levi
4.013 presumptuous
4.014 a. murmuring
b. serpents
4.015 true
4.016 false
4.017 false
4.018 true
4.019 true
4.020 true
4.021 false
4.022 true
4.023 true
4.024 false
4.025 d
4.026 g
4.027 a
4.028 l
4.029 e
4.030 j
4.031 h
4.032 k
4.033 f
4.034 b
4.035 c
4.036 a
4.037 e
4.038 b
4.039 e
4.040 a
4.041 c
4.042 a
4.043 b
4.044 b

LIFEPAC TEST

1. mercy seat
2. Ark of the Testimony (or Covenant)
3. altar of incense
4. table of shewbread
5. golden candlestick
6. laver
7. brazen altar
8. a
9. b
10. b
11. b
12. 27
13. obedience
14. 27-30
15. Levi
16. wilderness wanderings
17. b
18. f
19. a
20. c
21. e
22. true
23. true
24. true
25. false

ALTERNATE LIFEPAC TEST

1. c
2. e
3. k
4. h
5. j
6. a
7. f
8. i
9. b
10. g
11. false
12. true
13. true
14. true
15. true
16. false
17. true
18. Pi-hahiroth
19. Either order:
    a. manna
    b. quail
20. Either order:
    a. Marah
    b. Rephidim
21. a. fire
    b. cloud
22. Day of Atonement
23. Either order:
    a. Joshua
    b. Caleb
24. Any order:
    a. brazen altar
    b. lever
    c. table of shewbread
    d. golden lampstands
    e. mercy seat
    f. Ark of the Testimony
    g. altar of incense
25. Any order:
    a. in Egypt
    b. to Sinai
    c. at Sinai
26. Any order:
    a. burnt
    b. meal
    c. peace
    d. sin
    e. trespass

BIBLE 1003

ALTERNATE LIFEPAC TEST

NAME ______________________

DATE ______________________

SCORE ______________________

Match these items (each answer, 2 points).

1.	______	Hyksos	a.	rest
2.	______	Ra	b.	to draw out of the water
3.	______	Deuteronomy	c.	rulers of foreign lands
4.	______	Christ	d.	to expel
5.	______	Nazarite	e.	Egyptian sun god
6.	______	Sabbath	f.	Pharaoh
7.	______	Ahmose	g.	Ten Commandments
8.	______	Tabernacle	h.	our mercy seat
9.	______	Moses	i.	tent of meeting
10.	______	Decalogue	j.	a vow
			k.	second law

Answer true or false (each answer 1 point).

11. __________ The angel of death visited homes that had blood placed upon the door posts.

12. __________ A male lamb was slain at Passover.

13. __________ The moral law, given at Sinai, revealed the holiness of God.

14. __________ The ceremonial law, given at Sinai, revealed the work of Christ.

15. __________ The Levitical priest portrayed Christ as our High Priest.

16. ____________ The year of the Jubilee was observed every tenth year.

17. ____________ The tribes of Gad, Simeon, and Reuben assembled at the south of the Tabernacle.

Complete these statements (each answer, 3 points).

18. Prior to coming to the Red Sea, the Hebrews camped at ____________________ .

19. God provided food for the Hebrews in the form of a. ____________________ and b. ____________________ .

20. The Hebrews were without water at a. ____________________ and b. ____________________ .

21. God was with the children of Israel in the form of a pillar of a. ____________________ and a b. ____________________ .

22. The most significant day to Israel was the day of ____________________ .

23. Two of the spies sent out to survey the land that God had promised to Israel were a. ____________________ and b.____________________ .

Complete these activities (each answer, 3 points).

24. List seven items found within the Tabernacle.

a. ____________________ b. ____________________ c. ____________________

d. ____________________ e. ____________________ f ____________________

g. ____________________

25. List three geographical settings considered in this LIFEPAC.

a. ____________________ b. ____________________ c. ____________________

26. List the five Levitical offerings.

a. ____________________ b. ____________________ c. ____________________

d. ____________________ e. ____________________

BIBLE 1004

Unit 4: Israel in Canaan

TEACHER NOTES

MATERIALS NEEDED FOR LIFEPAC	
Required	Suggested
• none	• Bible, King James Version • other versions of the Bible if permitted • wall map of the Land of Israel during the time of the conquest of Joshua • Unger's or Halley's Bible handbook • Strong's, Young's, or a paperback Bible concordance • Bible dictionary • Bible atlas • commentaries on Joshua • *International Standard Bible Encyclopedia* or *Zondervan Pictorial Encyclopedia of the Bible* • the reference materials can be in either book or online formats

ADDITIONAL LEARNING ACTIVITIES

Section 1: Conquest of the Land

1. Discuss what God intended when He told Joshua to meditate in the Word both day and night (Joshua 1:8). Ask if this rule is only for Joshua or for all of God's people. Does this rule encourage daily study of the Bible?
2. Divide the classroom into a map of Canaan using desks and chairs as cities, rivers, and important landmarks. Have the students walk through the three campaigns of the conquest of the land. Identify each city and event as you go.
3. Have each member of a group find an alternate outline of the Biblical book of Joshua. Reassemble the group to form a master outline of the book.
4. Allow a group to gather the necessary materials to build the stone altars mentioned in Joshua chapter 4. Have the group explain the significance of each group of stones and why a more elaborate altar was not demanded by God.
5. Write a brief essay on Achan's sin. Use additional Scriptures to enhance your report.
6. Write a paper in which you compare the report of the two spies who returned from Jericho with the spies who are mentioned in Numbers 13:31–33. Answer the question of which group exercised faith and which group did not.

Section 2: Division of the Land

1. Discuss Rahab's apparent lie to the Jericho authorities and Achan's sin at Ai. Why was one dealt with harshly and the other not? Were they both wrong or was Rahab right in what she did?
2. Divide the class into thirteen groups and, using the class room as a map of Canaan, divide the land among the necessary tribes. Use a row of desks or chairs for the Jordan.
3. Using a hardening material such as a mixture of salt or flour and water, make a relief map of Canaan. Show the cities of the conquest and the division of the land.
4. Divide a group into different teams representing different tribes. Have the group debate or discuss who should be given which portion of the land.
5. You play the role of a Levite discovering you will not be getting any land. Write a letter to the editor of the *Canaan Times* stating your point of view. Use logic and reasoning in forming your argument.
6. Develop chapter titles in your own words for each of the twenty-four chapters of the book of Joshua. Make sure your titles are reasonable and logical. You may wish to display these titles on a poster in the classroom. See if you can memorize these titles.

Section 3: Farewell and Death of Joshua

1. 1. Read aloud Joshua's farewell in Joshua chapters 23 and 24. Have the students discuss the confidence a believer can have even as he faces death.
2. Discuss any similarities that might exist between Joshua and the Lord Jesus. Discuss the parallel between what Joshua did physically for God's people and what the Lord did in the spiritual realm.
3. Have the students trace the activities of the tribes of Israel following the death of Joshua. Have the students seek to identify the successful tribes and the unsuccessful tribes.
4. God did not give Israel a single strong leader after the death of Joshua. Have the students discuss this topic and compose a list of reasons why God did not give the Israelites a leader.
5. Using a good Bible concordance, find as many references as you can to Joshua in the books of the Bible other than the book of Joshua. Write out the location of these verses and make a list of any additional information you may learn.
6. Joshua had the Tabernacle set up at Shiloh. Using a Bible dictionary, handbook, concordance, or topical Bible, make a list of the places the Tabernacle went following the death of Joshua.

STUDENT WORKSHEET

The activity on the following page may be reproduced as a student worksheet.

» ANSWER KEY

RAHAB

BOAZ

OBED

JESSE

DAVID

SOLOMON

REHOBOAM

ABIJAH

ASA

JEHOSHAPHAT

JORAM

UZZIAH

JOTHAM

AHAZ

HEZEKIAH

Administer the LIFEPAC Test.
The test is to be administered in one session. Give no help except with directions.
Evaluate the tests and review areas where the students have done poorly.
Review the pages and activities that stress the concepts tested.
If necessary, administer the Alternate LIFEPAC Test.

» RAHAB THE HARLOT—A WOMAN OF GOD

Rahab the harlot, who sought the safety of the spies who came to Jericho, was saved by God and became a follower of Jehovah. She also became a part of the lineage of the Lord Jesus Christ. Using a concordance, Bible dictionary, Bible encyclopedia, or topical Bible, trace the family of Rahab. Follow the line through which Christ would eventually come. Continue this family tree to the time of Hezekiah, king of Judah. Use additional paper if necessary to complete this project.

ANSWER KEYS

SECTION 1

1.1 a. I. Conquest of the land (1 - 12)
b. II. Division of the land (13-22)
c. III. Farewell and death of Joshua (23-24)
1.2 history
1.3 Talmud
1.4 a. redemption
b. into
1.5 a. war
b. equipped or armed
1.6 a. iron
b. cities
1.7 a. alliances
b. common enemies
1.8 Any order:
a. God's charge to Joshua
b. the reconnaissance of Jericho
c. the crossing of Jordan
d. a spiritual renewal at Gilgal
1.9 a. to cross the Jordan
b. to conquer the land
c. to divide the inheritance
1.10 Example:
In Joshua 1:8, the Lord exhorted Joshua that prosperity and success were dependent upon careful meditation in and obedience to the book of the law.
1.11 Example:
Joshua 1:9, God encouraged Joshua to be strong, courageous, and fearless because Jehovah his God would be with him at all times and in every place.
1.12 Either order (a, b):
a. Reubenites
b. Gadites
c. Manasseh
1.13 reconnaissance
1.14 true
1.15 Either order:
a. David
b. Jesus
1.16 Gilgal
1.17 Any order:
a. Joshua was established among the people as Moses' successor.
b. Israel was assured of God's presence with them.
c. Israel was brought into the final stage of their redemptive experience: into the Promised Land.
d. The Canaanites were terrified by Israel.
1.18 Passover
1.19 a. circumcision
b. obedience
c. covenant (Abrahamic)
1.20 manna
1.21 a. Captain
b. Lord
1.22 victories (future)
1.23 Either order:
a. to conquer the land God had given them
b. to destroy and exterminate the wicked Canaanites, whose sin and idolatry God hated and would destroy
1.24 Either order:
a. Jericho
b. Ai
1.25 a. faith
b. obedience
1.26 Either order:
a. increased fear in the hearts of the people of Jericho
b. increased faith in the heart of the Israelites
1.27 massive walls
1.28 a. Rahab and her family
b. the silver, gold, brass, and iron
c. the Lord's treasury
1.29 a. Ai
b. sin
1.30 Achan
1.31 sin was judged
1.32 holy
1.33 a. Ebal
b. Gerizim
c. Moses

1.34 a. God
b. His word or proclaimed their allegiance to Him
1.35 Either order:
a. Gibeonites
b. Hivites
1.36 seek the Lord's counsel
1.37 a. hailstones
b. the length of day
c. time
1.38 a. north
b. Jabin
c. Hazor
1.39 a. God
b. destruction

SELF TEST 1

1.01 false
1.02 false
1.03 true
1.04 false
1.05 true
1.06 c
1.07 a
1.08 c
1.09 b
1.010 d
1.011 a. I. Conquest of the land (1-12)
b. II. Division of the land (13-22)
c. III. Farewell and death of Joshua (23-24)
1.012 Any order:
a. a charge to Joshua
b. the reconnaissance of Jericho
c. the crossing of Jordan
d. a spiritual renewal at Gilgal
1.013 Joshua
1.014 Either order:
a. to conquer the land God had given them
b. to destroy and exterminate the wicked Canaanites
1.015 e
1.016 d
1.017 f
1.018 a
1.019 c

SECTION 2

2.1 Moses
2.2 Any order:
a. the Reubenites
b. the Gadites
c. the half tribe of Manasseh
2.3 Levi
2.4 lot
2.5 Gilgal
2.6 a. Shiloh
b. Tabernacle
2.7 a. lot
b. size of the tribe
2.8 Caleb's
2.9 Joshua
2.10 Any order:
a. Benjamin
b. Simeon
c. Zebulun
d. Issachar
e. Asher
f. Naphtali
g. Dan
2. 11 center
2.12 Moses
2.13 anyone who has killed a person unintentionally
2.14 Any order:
a. Kadesh
b. Shechem
c. Hebron
2.15 Any order:
a. Bezer
b. Ramoth
c. Golan
2.16 forty-eight
2.17 refuge
2.18 true
2.19 a. suburbs
b. pastureland
2.20 a. (twelve) tribes
b. lot
2.21 Any order:
a. to love the Lord
b. to walk in His way
c. to keep His commandments
d. to cleave unto Him
e. to serve Him with all their heart and soul
2.22 altar
2.23 a. explanation
b. altar
2.24 a. Phinehas
b. ten
2.25 a. a good report
b. well received
2.26 It is a witness between us that Jehovah is God.

SELF TEST 2

2.01 true
2.02 false
2.03 true
2.04 true
2.05 false
2.06 false
2.07 true
2.08 g
2.09 e
2.010 i
2.011 f
2.012 h
2.013 c
2.014 b
2.015 d *or* a
2.016 a
2.017 d
2.018 b
2.019 a
2.020 b
2.021 a. Levites
b. lot
2.022 Jericho
2.023 manna
2.024 the Lord
2.025 a. twelve stones
b. Gilgal
2.026 sin
2.027 (great) altar
2.028 east
2.029 a. I. Conquest of the land (1-12)
b. II. Division of the land (13-22)
c. III. Farewell and death of Joshua (23-24)
2.030 Any order:
a. to love the Lord
b. to walk in His way
c. to keep His commandments
d. to cleave unto Him
e. to serve Him with all their heart and soul

SECTION 3

3.1 good things
3.2 evil things
3.3 possession
3.4 expulsion or removal
3.5 a. keep
b. do
3.6 renewed with them the covenant
3.7 Any order:
a. the Lord appeared there to Abraham and promised Canaan to His seed—Israel. Abraham also built an altar there.
b. Jacob built an altar at Shechem and called it El-elohe-Israel, the mighty God of Israel.
c. Israel and Joshua gathered there to fulfill the command of Moses in Moab to build an altar and write the Law on plastered stone.

SELF TEST 3

3.01 d
3.02 b
3.03 d
3.04 c
3.05 b
3.06 true
3.07 true
3.08 true
3.09 true
3.010 false
3.011 false
3.012 false
3.013 b
3.014 f
3.015 d
3.016 i
3.017 g
3.018 a
3.019 h
3.020 c
3.021 a. disobedience
b. obedience
3.022 a. redemption
b. Israel
3.023 Jericho
3.024 Captain
3.025 Any order:
a. to cross the Jordan
b. to conquer the land
c. to divide the inheritance
3.026 Jericho
3.027 Joshua's charge to Israel was to keep and to do all that is written in the book of the Law of Moses.
3.028 Any order:
a. to love the Lord
b. to walk in His way
c. to keep His commandments
d. to cleave to Him
e. to serve Him with all their heart and soul

LIFEPAC TEST

1. true
2. false
3. true
4. false
5. true
6. b
7. a
8. c
9. a
10. d
11. d
12. c
13. f
14. b
15. e
16. Any order:
a. the central campaign
b. the southern campaign
c. the northern campaign
17. a. I. Conquest of the land (1-12)
b. II. Division of the land (13-22)
c. III. Farewell and death of Joshua (23-24)
18. Shechem
19. a. sin
b. Achan
20. Talmud

ALTERNATE LIFEPAC TEST

1. d
2. g
3. f
4. h
5. k
6. e
7. a
8. j
9. i
10. c
11. false
12. false
13. true
14. true
15. true
16. false
17. true
18. false
19. true
20. false
21. Rahab
22. Shittim
23. Ai
24. Amorites
25. a. Egypt
b. Canaan
26. Moses
27. Gilgal
28. Joshua
29. Judah
30. a. Conquest of the Land
b. Division of the Land
c. Farewell and Death of Joshua
31. Any order:
a. cross the Jordan
b. conquer the land
c. divide the inheritance
32. a. central
b. southern
c. northern
33. Any order:
a. Manasseh
b. Gad
c. Reuben

BIBLE 1004

ALTERNATE LIFEPAC TEST

NAME ______________________________

DATE ______________________________

SCORE ______________________________

Match these items (each answer, 2 points).

1.	________	reconnaissance	a.	a token of the covenant
2.	________	Canaan	b.	a warrior
3.	________	Achan	c.	used to make a choice
4.	________	Kadesh	d.	preliminary survey
5.	________	Talmud	e.	Israel's half tribe
6.	________	Manasseh	f.	a thief
7.	________	circumcision	g.	the land
8.	________	Phinehas	h.	a city of refuge
9.	________	Shiloh	i.	location of the Tabernacle
10.	________	lots	j.	a priest
			k.	Jewish writings

Write true or false (each answer, 1 point).

11. ______________ Israel was required to wade across the Jordan.

12. ______________ Israel's first responsibility in the land was battle.

13. ______________ Jericho was a walled fortress west of the Jordan.

14. ______________ The tribe of Levi received no inheritance of land.

15. ______________ Joshua died at the age of 110 years.

16. ______________ Joshua was buried at Shechem.

17. ______________ The Levites were given forty-eight cities.

18. ____________ The first portion of the book of Joshua outlines the division of the land.

19. ____________ The king of Hazor was Jabin.

20. ____________ The Lord provided manna for the people of Israel once they entered the land.

Complete these statements (each answer, 3 points).

21. The harlot of Jericho who hid the two spies was ________________ .

22. Prior to coming to the Jordan, Israel camped at ________________ .

23. Israel's first defeat occurred at ________________ .

24. The sun and the moon stood still during Joshua's battle with the ________________ .

25. The redemptive theme of Joshua is, "out of a. ________________ and into b. ________________ ."

26. The division of the land east of the Jordan was first made by ________________ .

27. The tribes assembled to divide the land at ________________ .

28. The last person to receive an inheritance was ________________ .

29. The first tribe to receive its inheritance was ________________ .

Complete these activities (each answer, 3 points).

30. List in order the titles of the three major divisions of Joshua.

a. ________________ b. ________________ c. ________________

31. List the three commands God gave to Joshua.

a. ________________ b. ________________ c. ________________

32. List in order the three campaigns of Israel in the land.

a. ________________ b. ________________ c. ________________

33. List the three tribes that occupied the land east of the Jordan River.

a. ________________ b. ________________ c. ________________

BIBLE 1005

Unit 5: The Judges and Spiritual Decline

TEACHER NOTES

MATERIALS NEEDED FOR LIFEPAC	
Required	Suggested
• none	• Bible, King James Version • other versions of the Bible if permitted • Unger's or Halley's handbook of the Bible • Bible atlas • Bible dictionary • *International Standard Bible Encyclopedia* or *Zondervan Pictorial Encyclopedia of the Bible* • A wall map of the area of Israel during the days of the judges • the reference materials can be in either book or online formats

ADDITIONAL LEARNING ACTIVITIES

Section 1: The Book of Judges

1. Discuss the extent of the history of Israel from the death of Joshua to the time of Samuel. Too often this long period of time is seen as just a few years rather than over two centuries.
2. Discuss the purpose of divine discipline as illustrated by the cycles of the period of the judges. How do these relate to personal discipline that we receive from God today?
3. Have the students form small groups to debate whether Israel was better off under the judges or under the later kings. Was the freedom the Hebrews had during the time of the judges an asset or a detriment?
4. Have the students research if other nations have declined in the same manner as did Israel. Could the recurring cycles occur in our country today?
5. Make a time line of the period of the Judges and display it in the classroom.
6. Make a wall poster illustrating the cycles of discipline during the period of the judges. An example is given in the first section of the LIFEPAC.

Section 2: The History of the Judges

1. Divide the class into two teams and have a contest where the students are called upon to name the oppressors or the judges who restored order. A spelling exercise could also be included.
2. Discuss how God uses men. Talk about other men, besides the judges, who have been used by God. Ask the students if God has to or chooses to use men. Also discuss the character of the men God uses.
3. Have small groups of students chart out on large posters the cycles of discipline in the book of Judges. Have the students use the correct chronological order of these cycles.

4. Allow the students to write and perform skits that would portray any of the important events in the book of Judges.
5. Make a map of the Land of Israel that shows the area of influence of each of the judges.
6. You have studied how God used Deborah as a judge. Make a list of other women in the Old Testament whom God used. Find the passages that speak of these women of God and list on a paper their names, areas of influence, and the time in which they lived.
7. After completing the study of Section 2, have the students write a 300-word report on one of the judges. This report should use additional sources, and a concordance should be used to check other biblical references to the judge selected.

Section 3: Two Examples of Decay

1. Discuss the importance of doing exactly what the Lord tells us to do. Discuss how spiritual decline begins with ignoring the Word of God.
2. Parallel the moral and spiritual decay of Israel with the decay of our country today. If God disciplined Israel, will He not also deal justly with error today?
3. Have the students discuss what should have been done to punish the Levite who took the concubine. Consider his crime in the light of Old Testament and modern-day law.
4. Have the students break up into small groups to make charts or wall posters showing the idolatry of the Israelites throughout the Old Testament history. At the top of the poster put the words of Exodus 20:4.
5. Write a paper on the idolatry that is found in our culture today. Consider the many things that people, even Christian people, put between themselves and their relationship with the Lord.
6. Make a time line chart that plots the decay of Israel during the period of the judges.

Section 4: The Story of Ruth

1. Discuss the nobility of both Ruth and Boaz. Compare their actions to what a young couple in love might have done today if in a similar situation.
2. Discuss with the students how God will often direct us through circumstances. Use Ruth as an example. Ask the students to share examples they may have. When God closes one door, He often opens another.
3. Divide a group into two teams and have one team assume Naomi's bitter attitude and the other team portray Ruth's faithful and loving attitude. Have the group discuss their sojourn in Moab and their return to Bethlehem.
4. Divide the students into groups and have them write and perform the events of the book of Ruth in skits.
5. Make a chart that shows the family line from Ruth and Boaz to Solomon. This chart may be displayed in the classroom.
6. Do a dramatic reading or oral interpretation of one of the rich passages from the book of Ruth.
7. Write a paper in which you compare the Kinsman-Redeemer to the redemption wrought by the Lord Jesus Christ.

STUDENT WORKSHEET

The activity on the following page may be reproduced as a student worksheet.

» ANSWER KEY

1. Othniel
2. Ehud
3. Shamgar
4. Deborah
5. Gideon
6. Tola
7. Jair
8. Jephthah
9. Ibzan
10. Elon
11. Abdon
12. Samson

Any reasonable title will meet the requirements of their assignment.

Administer the LIFEPAC Test.
The test is to be administered in one session. Give no help except with directions.
Evaluate the tests and review areas where the students have done poorly.
Review the pages and activities that stress the concepts tested.
If necessary, administer the Alternate LIFEPAC Test.

» THE DISTRESSING DAYS OF THE JUDGES

Many notable men of God served the Lord as judges between the time of Joshua and Samuel. Now that you have studied these men, see if you can arrange their names in the proper chronological order. Try to complete this activity without using any references. After you have completed this activity, check your answers with the Chart of the Judges in Section 1 of this LIFEPAC and list the corrections in the third column.

THE JUDGES	THEIR ORDER	CORRECTIONS
Abdon	1. ____________	____________
Deborah	2. ____________	____________
Ehud	3. ____________	____________
Elon	4. ____________	____________
Gideon	5. ____________	____________
Ibzan	6. ____________	____________
Jair	7. ____________	____________
Jephthah	8. ____________	____________
Othniel	9. ____________	____________
Samson	10. ____________	____________
Shamgar	11. ____________	____________
Tola	12. ____________	____________

One Biblical scholar has called this period of Israel's history the "Distressing Days of the Judges." What would you call this black period of Israel's past?

____

ANSWER KEYS

SECTION 1

1.1 introduction
1.2 drive out the Canaanites completely
1.3 a. valley
b. chariots of iron
1.4 a. lack of faith in God
b. lack of obedience to His command or disobedience
1.5 taxation
1.6 a. thorns in Israel's sides
b. a snare to Israel
1.7 history
1.8 a. apostasy
b. servitude
1.9 preview
1.10 shophetim
1.11 a. apostasy
b. servitude
c. repentance
d. deliverance
1.12 foreign oppressors
1.13 Either order:
a. deliver
b. govern
1.14 Either order:
a. times of oppression
b. times of servitude

SELF TEST 1

1.01 false
1.02 true
1.03 true
1.04 false
1.05 true
1.06 d
1.07 b
1.08 a
1.09 c
1.010 d
1.011 a. twelve
b. history
1.012 possession
1.013 a. Joshua
b. Samuel
1.014 a. 1. THE BOOK OF JUDGES
Judges 1:1-3:4
b. 2. THE HISTORY OF JUDGES
Judges 3:5-16:31
c. 3. TWO EXAMPLES OF DECAY
Judges 17-21
d. 4. THE STORY OF RUTH
Ruth 1-4
1.015 background

SECTION 2

2.1 twelve

2.2 a. to serve as military leader during the war for freedom
b. to govern during the following period of freedom

2.3 Any order:
a. Canaanites
b. Hittites
c. Amorites
d. Perizzites
e. Hivites
f. Jebusites

2.4 a. Chushan-rishathaim
b. Mesopotamia
c. eight

2.5 a. Othniel
b. Caleb

2.6 God

2.7 the anointing of the Spirit

2.8 God

2.9 forty

2.10 the Israelites did evil in the sight of the Lord

2.11 a. Eglon
b. Moab

2.12 Jericho

2.13 eighteen

2.14 Ehud

2.15 a. Jordan
b. Moab

2.16 a. eighty
b. Philistines

2.17 a. Philistines
b. Shamgar
c. Philistines or men
d. ox goad

2.18 "did evil in the sight of the Lord"

2.19 a. Canaanites
b. twenty

2.20 900

2.21 cried unto the Lord for deliverance

2.22 Deborah

2.23 Barak

2.24 a. the Lord
b. Barak
c. Israel

2.25 Jael

2.26 seven

2.27 Any order (b-d):
a. dens
b. mountains
c. caves
d. strongholds

2.28 a. economic
b. military

2.29 locusts

2.30 prophet

2.31 Gideon

2.32 fire

2.33 Either order:
a. dew
b. dryness

2.34 a. Jehovah-shalom
b. Jehovah is peace

2.35 a. tear down the altar of Baal
b. offer a sacrifice with the wood of the grove

2.36 Baal

2.37 Any order:
a. Manasseh
b. Asher
c. Zebulun
d. Naphtali

2.38 Manasseh

2.39 He was instructed to do so by the Lord to demonstrate the Lord's strength.

2.40 a. the Lord
b. Gideon
c. army (of 300 men)

2.41 Either order:
a. torch (in an empty pitcher)
b. trumpet

2.42 dream

2.43 a. torches
b. trumpets

2.44 Either order:
a. frighten
b. confuse

2.45 forty

2.46 Tola

2.47 Issachar

2.48 twenty-three years

2.49 Jair

2.50 twenty-two years

2.51 Gilead

2.52 Israel was apparently at peace and without oppression.

2.53 Any order:
a. Baalim
b. Ashtaroth
c. the gods of Syria
d. the gods of Sidon
e. the gods of Moab
f. the gods of the Ammonites
g. the gods of the Philistines

2.54 Either order:
a. Philistines
b. Ammonites
2.55 valour
2.56 negotiate
2.57 delivered to Israel by the Lord from the Amorites, not the Ammonites
2.58 the Lord
2.59 a. virginity
b. death
2.60 Any order:
a. Ibzan
b. Elon
c. Abdon
2.61 twenty-five
2.62 Philistines
2.63 forty
2.64 Ammonites
2.65 Philistines
2.66 a son
2.67 burnt offering
2.68 fire
2.69 Timnath
2.70 a. power
b. weakness
2.71 Samson slew thirty Philistines at Ashkelon and took their garments.
2.72 jawbone of a donkey
2.73 a. weakness
b. strength
2.74 a. Hebron
b. west
2.75 Delilah
2.76 uncut hair
2.77 the Lord departed from him
2.78 a. put out his eyes
b. made him grind their grain in a prison gristmill
2.79 Dagon
2.80 true
2.81 true
2.82 true

SELF TEST 2

2.01 c
2.02 a
2.03 b
2.04 a
2.05 d
2.06 f
2.07 h
2.08 e
2.09 b
2.010 a
2.011 g
2.012 c *or* e
2.013 a. Israel
b. land
2.014 a. 1. THE BOOK OF JUDGES
Judges 1:1-3:4
b. 2. THE HISTORY OF JUDGES
Judges 3:5-16:31
c. 3. TWO EXAMPLES OF DECAY
Judges 17-21
d. 4. THE STORY OF RUTH
Ruth 1-4
2.015 a. to serve as military leader during the war for freedom
b. to govern during the following period of freedom
2.016 apostasy, servitude, repentance, and deliverance
2.017 The Israelites did evil in the sight of the Lord
2.018 God commanded Gideon to tear down the altar of Baal and to offer a sacrifice with the wood of the grove.
2.019 Israel served (in any order) Baalim, Ashtaroth, the gods of Syria, the gods of Sidon, the gods of Moab, the gods of the Ammonites, and the gods of the Philistines.
2.020 Example:
The error of the Ammonite king that Jephthah pointed out was that the land in question had been delivered to Israel by the Lord from the Amorites, not the Ammonites.

SECTION 3

3.1 a. the fact that Micah "called" the Levite to serve as his priest
b. the fact that the Levite accepted the "call" of Micah to serve as his priest

3.2 Example:
They sent a spying mission to find another territory for settlement because they, having failed to take possession of their inheritance, were experiencing difficulties with the Amorites.

3.3 They found Laish an inviting, secluded place that would be easily conquered.

3.4 They robbed the sanctuary of Micah and persuaded his Levite to join their expedition.

3.5 They set up their stolen images, instituted an idolatrous system of worship, and established Micah's Levite as their priest.

3.6 God was no longer Israel's king

3.7 a. Levite
b. priesthood
c. Tabernacle worship

3.8 Gibeah

3.9 Benjamin

3.10 a. twice
b. Benjamites

3.11 a. They asked counsel of the Lord.
b. They wept before the Lord.
c. They fasted and offered burnt offerings and peace offerings before the Lord.

3.12 the Lord

3.13 six hundred

3.14 a. Jabesh-Gilead
b. death
c. four hundred

3.15 Shiloh

SELF TEST 3

3.01 true

3.02 false

3.03 false

3.04 false

3.05 true

3.06 d

3.07 a

3.08 c

3.09 d

3.010 b

3.011 a. Levite
b. Gibeah

3.012 a. victory
b. Lord
c. (the tribe of) Benjamin

3.013 a. deliver
b. judge

3.014 every man does what is right in his own eyes

3.015 God was no longer Israel's king

3.016 Mizpah

3.017 a. the fact that Micah "called" the Levite to serve as his priest
b. the fact that the Levite accepted the "call" of Micah to serve as his priest

3.018 Example:
They sent a spying mission to find another territory for settlement because they, having failed to take possession of their inheritance, were experiencing difficulties with the Amorites.

3.019 They found Laish an inviting, secluded place that would be easily conquered.

3.020 They robbed the sanctuary of Micah and persuaded his Levite to join their expedition.

3.021 They set up their stolen images, instituted an idolatrous system of worship, and established Micah's Levite as their priest.

SECTION 4

4.1 a. genealogy
b. David
c. Christ

4.2 suffering or distress or famine

4.3 a. husband
b. sons

4.4 her homeland

4.5 a. Orpah
b. Ruth

4.6 spiritual

4.7 a. Boaz
b. Elimelech

4.8 the Mosaic Law

4.9 A kinsman-redeemer was a brother or next of kin to a man who died without sons, who should redeem the dead man's property and marry his widow.

4.10 "Rest" meant a dwelling place in the home of a husband.

4.11 He must publicly release his claim, and the next nearest kinsman could then take his place as kinsman-redeemer.

4.12 Obed was the grandfather of David and the ancestor of Christ.

SELF TEST 4

4.01 true
4.02 true
4.03 false
4.04 true
4.05 false
4.06 d
4.07 b
4.08 a
4.09 b
4.010 d

4.011 a. 1. THE BOOK OF JUDGES
Judges 1:1-3:4
b. 2. THE HISTORY OF JUDGES
Judges 3:5-16:31
c. 3. TWO EXAMPLES OF DECAY
Judges 17-21
d. 4. THE STORY OF RUTH
Ruth 1-4

4.012 a. Moab
b. husband
c. sons

4.013 the famine was ended in Judah
4.014 Levite
4.015 shophetim or judges

4.016 Any order:
a. He would not drive the Canaanites out of the land.
b. The Canaanites would become thorns in Israel's sides.
c. The Canaanite gods would become a snare to Israel.

4.017 "Rest" meant a dwelling place in the home of a husband.

4.018 A kinsman-redeemer was a brother or next of kin to a man who died without sons, who should redeem the dead man's property and marry his widow.

4.019 He must publicly release his claim, and the next nearest kinsman could then take his place as kinsman-redeemer.

4.020 Obed was the grandfather of David and the ancestor of Christ.

4.021 Gideon
4.022 Jephthah
4.023 Ehud
4.024 Shamgar
4.025 Samson

LIFEPAC TEST

1. a
2. b
3. d
4. b
5. c
6. false
7. true
8. false
9. true
10. true
11. true
12. false
13. remain in Moab
14. a. Micah
    b. Danites
15. Either order:
    a. redeem the dead man's property
    b. marry his widow
16. to find a dwelling place in the home of a husband
17. a. David
    b. Christ
18. spiritual
19. moral or spiritual
20. a. 1. THE BOOK OF JUDGES
    Judges 1:1-3:4
    b. 2. THE HISTORY OF JUDGES
    Judges 3:5-16:31
    c. 3. TWO EXAMPLES OF DECAY
    Judges 17-21
    d. 4. THE STORY OF RUTH
    Ruth 1-4
21. a. the fact that Micah "called" the Levite to serve as his priest
    b. the fact that the Levite accepted the "call" to serve as his priest
22. Example:
    The error of the Ammonite king that Jephthah pointed out was that the land in question had been delivered to Israel by the Lord from the Amorites, not the Ammonites.
23. d
24. a
25. f
26. b
27. c
28. e
29. e
30. a

ALTERNATE LIFEPAC TEST

1. c
2. g
3. k
4. i
5. a
6. f
7. d
8. h
9. j
10. e
11. true
12. false
13. true
14. true
15. true
16. false
17. true
18. true
19. true
20. false
21. a. sin
    b. servitude
    c. repentance
    d. deliverance
22. Either order:
    a. Danites
    b. the crime of Gibeah
23. Either order:
    a. Mahlon
    b. Chilon
24. a. judge
    b. a near relative who redeems the property and widow of one who has died
25. Deborah
26. Moabites
27. Philistines
28. judges
29. Caleb
30. jawbone
31. Delilah

BIBLE 1005

ALTERNATE LIFEPAC TEST

NAME ______________________

DATE ______________________

SCORE ______________________

Match these items (each answer, 2 points).

1. ______ Ehud
2. ______ Jephthah
3. ______ Elon
4. ______ Samson
5. ______ Othniel
6. ______ Jair
7. ______ Shamgar
8. ______ Abdon
9. ______ Tola
10. ______ Gideon

a. Caleb's nephew
b. a Levite
c. an assassin
d. used an ox goad
e. given signs
f. had thirty sons
g. vowed a vow
h. had forty sons
i. A Nazarite from birth
j. from the tribe of Issachar
k. from the tribe of Zebulun

Write true or false (each answer, 1 point).

11. __________ The period of the judges ended with Israel in decay.
12. __________ Micah forsook idolatry to worship Jehovah.
13. __________ Many men in Gibeah were degenerates.
14. __________ The Benjamite was small but well trained.
15. __________ Ruth was a Moabitess.
16. __________ Ruth's attitude was one of bitterness when she returned to Bethlehem.
17. __________ Boaz was a kinsman of Elimelech.

18. ____________ Boaz was the son of Rahab.

19. ____________ Israel failed to drive out their enemies after the death of Joshua.

20. ____________ Ruth was the grandmother of Saul.

Complete these activities (each answer, 3 points).

21. List in their correct order the four recurring cycles of the period of the judges.

a. ______________________ b. ______________________

c. ______________________ d. ______________________

22. List the two examples of decay in Israel.

a. ______________________ b. ______________________

23. List the two sons of Elimelech.

a. ______________________ b. ______________________

Define these words (each answer, 5 points).

24. a. shophetim ______________________

b. kinsman-redeemer ______________________

Complete these statements (each answer, 3 points).

25. The only woman judge was ______________________ .

26. Ehud defeated the ______________________ .

27. Samson defeated the ______________________ .

28. The story of Ruth occurred within the period of the ______________________ .

29. The one who drove the Anakims from Israel was ______________________ .

30. Samson slew a thousand men with the ______________________ of a donkey.

31. Samson's hair was cut by the woman ______________________ .

BIBLE 1006

Unit 6: The Kingdom

TEACHER NOTES

MATERIALS NEEDED FOR LIFEPAC	
Required	Suggested
• none	• Bible, King James Version • other versions of the Bible if permitted • a wall map of the Land of Israel during the kingdom period • Unger's or Halley's Bible handbook • Bible atlas • Bible concordance • *International Standard Bible Encyclopedia* or *Zondervan Pictorial Encyclopedia of the Bible* • Bible commentaries • the reference materials can be in either book or online formats

ADDITIONAL LEARNING ACTIVITIES

Section 1: The Books of Samuel

1. Discuss the problems that occurred in Israel when the people did not have a king. Although this period was one of great freedom when God was their ruler, the people could not handle the freedom. Emphasize that with freedom comes responsibility.
2. Using a wall map or by making the classroom into a map of the Land of Israel, walk through the important military campaigns or travels of Samuel, Saul, David, or Solomon.
3. Allow a group of students to produce a skit that will portray any of the events mentioned in Section 1 of this LIFEPAC. Have the students write a script, select a cast, and perform the play for other students.
4. Have a group of students make a number of posters, charts, and time lines that will compare the reign of Saul with the reign of David.
5. Write a paper on Samuel's activities in each of his three offices—prophet, priest, and judge over Israel. You may also wish to illustrate your report.
6. You have learned that David's motive was right but that his method was wrong in returning the Ark from Kirjath-jearim. Make a list of normal activities that the Christian may engage in today and indicate how the means do not justify the ends—how our methods can also be wrong.

Section 2: The Kingdom under Solomon

1. Discuss the value of wisdom. Emphasis should be placed upon the wisdom and understanding that is available to the child of God as he studies the Bible. Give examples of various situations that the students may encounter and have the students determine the wisest solution.
2. Discuss Solomon's reversion and how, with all his wealth, he concluded that all was vanity. Emphasis in the discussion should be placed upon the error of thinking that riches bring happiness.
3. Have the students produce skits that will portray any of the important events in Solomon's life.
4. Have groups of students make a model of the Temple constructed by Solomon.
5. Using a concordance, find as many New Testament verses as time allows on the subject of wisdom. Then write a brief paper on the New Testament view of wisdom.
6. Write a paper on the glory, wealth, and power of Solomon. List his various assets, building projects, and family. Attempt to show as much as possible about his position and power.
7. Make a time line that shows the various important events in the life of Solomon.
8. Have the students write a 500–word report on either Samuel, Saul, David, or Solomon. The report should incorporate additional sources and integrate biblical material. An outline should first be prepared by the student and checked by the teacher to determine a logical flow of thought.

Section 3: The Hebrew Poetry

1. Select a number of good English poems and read them to the class. Discuss with the class the differences between our poetry and Hebrew poetry.
2. Using the book of Job as a text, discuss the reasons Christians suffer. Debate whether all suffering is bad or good, if some suffering is self-induced and other suffering is from God. Have the class list the numerous sources of suffering.
3. Have groups of students produce skits that portray the encounter of Job with the three comforters. In the script include the words of wisdom from Elihu.
4. Have groups of students make a number of different posters that help explain the book of Psalms. These posters can explain the divisions of the book, the types of Psalms, and the different parallelisms found in the Psalms.
5. Using the last chapter of Proverbs as a text, divide the students into small groups and discuss and debate the role of the Christian woman in our society.
6. Write a paper that will explain the various interpretations of the Song of Solomon. Use additional sources for this report.
7. Using the information you have gained from this LIFEPAC, study either Psalm 23, 100, or 150 and identify the types of parallelisms employed by the writer.

STUDENT WORKSHEET

The activity on the following page may be reproduced as a student worksheet.

» ANSWER KEY

Any fifteen New Testament quotes from the Psalms will satisfy the requirements of this assignment.

Administer the LIFEPAC Test.

The test is to be administered in one session. Give no help except with directions.
Evaluate the tests and review areas where the students have done poorly.
Review the pages and activities that stress the concepts tested.
If necessary, administer the Alternate LIFEPAC Test.

» THE PSALMS AND THE NEW TESTAMENT

Using a Bible concordance, a topical Bible, or a chain-reference Bible, find at least fifteen quotations of the Psalms in the books of the New Testament. On these lines list the verse from the Psalm that is used and then write the location of the verse in the New Testament where the verse is used.

	PSALMS	NEW TESTAMENT
1.	______________________	______________________
2.	______________________	______________________
3.	______________________	______________________
4.	______________________	______________________
5.	______________________	______________________
6.	______________________	______________________
7.	______________________	______________________
8.	______________________	______________________
9.	______________________	______________________
10.	______________________	______________________
11.	______________________	______________________
12.	______________________	______________________
13.	______________________	______________________
14.	______________________	______________________
15.	______________________	______________________

Name two New Testament authors who quote from the Psalms.

____

ANSWER KEYS

SECTION 1

1.1 one book
1.2 a. divided
b. Greek
c. Hebrew
1.3 a. the ministry of Samuel
b. the reign of Saul
c. the reign of David
1.4 Any order:
a. the cessation of sanctuary worship and service
b. the corruption of the priesthood
c. the widespread practice of idolatry
1.5 the godlessness and wicked deeds of the sons of Eli
1.6 a. theocracy
b. monarchy
1.7 Either order:
a. Hannah
b. Elkanah
1.8 asked of God
1.9 Shiloh
1.10 Speak, Lord; for Thy servant heareth.
1.11 a. confirmed his priestly ministry
b. called him to a prophetic ministry
1.12 a. judge
b. prophet
1.13 a. cart
b. milk cows
c. calves
1.14 Samuel
1.15 true
1.16 Examples (any order):
a. Samuel's sons, whom he had in error appointed as judges over Israel, were greedy and dishonest; they accepted bribes and perverted judgment.
b. The Ammonites were threatening Israel from the east.
c. Israel wanted to be like other nations around them who had kings.
1.17 Examples (any order):
a. He would meet two men by Rachel's sepulchre at Zelzah who would inform him about the donkeys and his father.
b. He would then meet three men in the plain of Tabor on their way to worship at Bethel carrying three kids, three loaves of bread, and a bottle of wine; they would give him two loaves of bread.
c. He would then encounter a company of prophets at the hill of God by the garrison of the Philistines, the Spirit of the Lord would come upon him, and he would prophesy.
1.18 a. premature
b. incorrect or wrong
1.19 a. theocracy
b. Jehovah(as their King)
1.20 a. Jehovah
b. Samuel
1.21 a. spiritual
b. political
1.22 Ramah
1.23 Benjamin
1.24 anointed him to be king
1.25 Mizpeh
1.26 a. a military victory
b. Ammonites
1.27 Either order:
a. humility
b. self-control
1.28 Jabesh-Gilead
1.29 right eyes put out
1.30 Example:
cutting to pieces a yoke of oxen and sending the pieces throughout the land with the warning that those men who did not respond by following Saul and Samuel would have the same thing happen to their oxen
1.31 a. Israel
b. Judah
1.32 Lord
1.33 b
1.34 e
1.35 a
1.36 d

1.37 a. storm
b. thunder
c. rain
d. sin
e. king
1.38 a. offer the sacrifice himself
b. Samuel
1.39 repentance
1.40 Amalekites
1.41 Example:
he spared Agag the king and the best of their flocks, herds, and goods
1.42 a. erect a memorial to himself
b. commemorate his victory
1.43 hypocritical
1.44 a. insincere
b. blame the people for his own sin
1.45 a. Jesse or Bethlehem
b. David
1.46 b
1.47 c
1.48 a
1.49 a *or* b
1.50 false
1.51 false
1.52 false
1.53 true
1.54 true
1.55 true
1.56 false
1.57 true
1.58 true
1.59 true
1.60 true
1.61 Hebron
1.62 Abner
1.63 Joab
1.64 a. Abner
b. Michal
1.65 Joab
1.66 a. Hebron
b. David
1.67 the location of the capital in a suitable city
1.68 a. enemy stronghold
b. never been taken
1.69 Abraham
1.70 tunnel or underground spring
1.71 a. Jerusalem
b. tunnel
1.72 a. assurance
b. following
c. attack
1.73 a. Ark
b. Kirjath-jearim
1.74 three
1.75 his function was warfare
1.76 a. confirm the royal authority for his house and family forever
b. fulfilled in Christ
1.77 son (Solomon)
1.78 Example:
The Ark should have been brought back and restored to a central place in the worship of Israel; but it should have been carried by the Levities, not transported upon a cart.
1.79 sins
1.80 a. sins
b. examples
1.81 Any order:
a. Tamar's forced incest with Amnon
b. Amnon's murder by Absalom
c. Absalom's revolt against David
d. Absalom's death by Joab

SELF TEST 1

1.01 d
1.02 c
1.03 c
1.04 d
1.05 a
1.06 true
1.07 true
1.08 true
1.09 false
1.010 true
1.011 music
1.012 a. (giant) Goliath
b. an errand
c. his father (Jesse)
1.013 a. Merab
b. he served in Saul's army
1.014 witchcraft
1.015 Hebron
1.016 a. location of the capital
b. suitable city
1.017 Example:
The Ark should have been brought back and restored to a central place in the worship of Israel; but it should have been carried by two priests, not transported upon a cart.
1.018 by the godlessness and wicked deeds of the sons of Eli
1.019 Any order:
judge, priest, and prophet
1.020 Example:
God had said that Israel would have kings, but He had not revealed when He would establish the kingdom. Israel should have waited for that revelation. Israel was demonstrating a disintegration of the theocracy—a rejection of Jehovah as their King. They wanted to be like other nations around them that had kings.

SECTION 2

2.1 false
2.2 false
2.3 true
2.4 true
2.5 false
2.6 false
2.7 true
2.8 true
2.9 false
2.10 true
2.11 Either order:
a. military victories
b. spiritual renewal
2.12 a. Gibeon
b. dream
2.13 give him
2.14 a. humility
b. his desire
c. wisdom
2.15 a. need
b. concern
2.16 Either order:
a. riches
b. honor or long life for faithful service
2.17 a. harlots or women
b. mother
c. child
2.18 a. sword
b. division
c. child
2.19 a. mother
b. child
c. life
2.20 a. child
b. mother
2.21 b
2.22 d
2.23 c
2.24 a. war
b. peace
2.25 a. peace (of)
b. victories
c. David
2.26 a. twelve
b. officers
2.27 Any order:
a. wisdom
b. wealth
c. honor
2.28 fourth
2.29 Tabernacle

2.30 a. stone
b. cedar
c. gold

2.31 The Ark of the Covenant was brought by the priests to the Temple and was placed in the Holy of Holies.

2.32 Example:
The general content of the prayer was that Jehovah might hear all those who call on Him, praying toward that place, and that He might forgive.

2.33 a. the time when Gentiles would call upon the Lord (8:41-43)
b. the time of Israel's exile (8:46-47)

2.34 "That all the people of the earth may know that the Lord is God, and that there is none else."

2.35 Example:
They were similar to those of the Tabernacle, but their size and number were different.

2.36 thirteen

2.37 Either order:
a. fortresses
b. store cities

2.38 hear the wisdom

2.39 a. hear
b. wisdom
c. God had put in his heart

2.40 the half had not been told her

2.41 20,000,000

2.42 ivory

2.43 a. silver
b. stones

2.44 The Lord was angry with Solomon because his heart was turned away from Him by his wives.

2.45 Ten tribes would go to Jeroboam, leaving two tribes for Solomon's son, Rehoboam.

2.46 Example:
Solomon sought to slay Jeroboam, God's appointed successor in the divided kingdom, even as Saul had sought to slay David, Solomon's father.

2.47 forty years

SELF TEST 2

2.01 true

2.02 true

2.03 false

2.04 true

2.05 true

2.06 a. Ark of the Covenant
b. Temple or Holy of Holies

2.07 a. the time when the Gentiles would call upon the Lord (8:41-43)
b. the time of Israel's exile (8:46-47)

2.08 silver

2.09 forty

2.010 a. Ministry of Samuel; 1 Samuel 1-7
b. Reign of Saul; 1 Samuel 8-31
c. Reign of David 2 Samuel 1-24

2.011 a. priestly
b. prophetic

2.012 e

2.013 d

2.014 a

2.015 b

2.016 Example:
Solomon's first recorded application of his wisdom from God involved two women who claimed to be the mother of one living child. To determine the true mother, Solomon requested a sword and commanded the division of the child between the two women. The true mother identified herself, as Solomon anticipated, by relinquishing her claim on the child. She was declared the real mother by Solomon and was given the child.

2.017 "That all the people of the earth may know that the Lord is God, and that there is none else."

2.018 Jesus said that the "queen of the south" came to hear Solomon's wisdom, which God had put in his heart.

SECTION 3

3.1 b
3.2 e
3.3 a
3.4 d
3.5 poetry
3.6 a. Uz
b. Edom
3.7 a. Uz
b. Edomites
3.8 Either order:
a. Noah
b. Daniel
3.9 patriarchal
3.10 Either order:
a. David
b. Solomon
3.11 Any order:
a. Job's riches were expressed in terms of animals and servants.
b. Job offered sacrifices as the head of his family.
c. A piece of money called a *qesitah* was used by both Job and Jacob.
d. The length of Job's life was similar to that of the patriarchs.
e. The expression used to describe Job's latter years was used similarly with reference to Abraham and Isaac.
f. In the book of Job, no reference is made either to the history of Israel or to the Law of Moses.
3.12 a. an exemplary man
b. defeat
3.13 faith
3.14 three
3.15 Any order:
a. Eliphaz
b. Bildad
c. Zophar
3.16 Either order:
a. Elihu
b. Job
3.17 a. vindication
b. restoration
c. twofold
3.18 Example:
Each friend argued that Job had sinned greatly and that his severe suffering was a direct result of that sin.
3.19 Example:
Job defended himself on the grounds of his personal integrity; he maintained that he was innocent of any wrongdoing.
3.20 Example:
Elihu took issue with Job's friends for their unwarranted accusations and with Job for his equally unwarranted self-righteousness.
3.21 Job's response was one of humble submission and penitent confession.
3.22 c
3.23 g
3.24 d
3.25 i
3.26 j
3.27 a
3.28 h
3.29 f
3.30 b
3.31 antithetic
3.32 synthetic
3.33 synonymous
3.34 antithetic
3.35 climactic
3.36 Resurrection
3.37 22
3.38 Hebrews 2:12
3.39 hated without cause
3.40 109
3.41 false
3.42 false
3.43 true
3.44 true
3.45 true
3.46 David feigned insanity to escape Achish
3.47 51
3.48 2 Samuel 15:13–16:14
3.49 52
3.50 2 Samuel 22
3.51 c
3.52 e

3.53 b
3.54 f
3.55 a
3.56 Solomon
3.57 a. couplet
b. parallelism
3.58 antithetic parallelism
3.59 a. couplet
b. verses
3.60 poem
3.61 a. introduction
b. book
3.62 a. to know wisdom and instruction
b. to perceive the words of understanding
3.63 Example:
Its purpose is to provide experiential knowledge and the ability to skillfully apply that knowledge (wisdom) and to be able to perceive wise sayings.
3.64 a. theme
b. the fear of the Lord
3.65 a. Solomon
b. Hezekiah's men
3.66 a. numerical
b. poetic
3.67 a. mother
b. justice
3.68 acrostic
3.69 a. wise
b. fears the Lord
3.70 the poor
3.71 The Hebrew title of Ecclesiastes is "The Discourses (Words) of Qoheleth (or Koheleth)."
3.72 "Ecclesiastes" is the Greek (Septuagint) translation of "Qoheleth."
3.73 Any order:
a. Solomon was the unrivaled wise man among the kings of Israel.
b. He was zealous in his search for wisdom and truth.
c. His wealth was unequaled.
d. His building projects were extensive.
e. His collection of proverbs was very large.
3.74 "All is vanity."
3.75 Examples:
a. Discourse I—things of this world don't bring happiness—only God's grace does
b. Discourse II—earthly success is joy with gratitude; 3-fold means for happiness is duty toward God, neighbors and ourselves
c. Discourse III—practical wisdom comes not by earthly sources, but through the fear of God
d. Discourse IV—true happiness comes by unfeigned faith in God and a life of faithfulness
3.76 Either order:
a. "All is vanity.'"
b. "Fear God and keep His commandments."
3.77 1,005
3.78 a. husband
b. wife
c. God or Christ
d. Israel or the Church or His people
3.79 a. literal
b. typical
3.80 a. typical
b. God and Israel
c. Christ and His Church

SELF TEST 3

3.01 b
3.02 d
3.03 d
3.04 a
3.05 b
3.06 true
3.07 true
3.08 false
3.09 true
3.010 true
3.011 Proverbs
3.012 Psalms
3.013 a. Tehillim
b. praises or songs of praises
3.014 a. priestly
b. prophetic
3.015 Amalekites
3.016 480th
3.017 music
3.018 antithetic
3.019 Job's response was one of humble submission and penitent confession.
3.020 synthetic parallelism
3.021 to know wisdom and instruction, and to perceive the words of understanding
3.022 Any order:
a. Solomon was the unrivaled wise man among the kings of Israel.
b. He was zealous in his search for wisdom and truth.
c. His wealth was unequaled.
d. His building projects were extensive.
e. His collection of proverbs was very large.
3.023 Example:
The purpose of The Song of Solomon is to honor the intimate love relationship between husband and wife, which typically parallels the relationship between God and His people.

LIFEPAC TEST

1. b
2. d
3. c
4. d
5. b
6. true
7. true
8. true
9. false
10. false
11. a. divided
b. Greek
c. Hebrew
12. a. the ministry of Samuel
b. the reign of Saul
c. the reign of David
13. Any order:
a. wisdom
b. wealth
c. honor
14. sins
15. i
16. e
17. h
18. c
19. b
20. k
21. d
22. f
23. j
24. g
25. "That all the people of the earth may know that the Lord is God, and that there is none else."
26. Example:
Things of this world which are apart from God do not bring happiness—only emptiness (answer should include this basic concept).

ALTERNATE LIFEPAC TEST

1. e
2. f
3. h
4. j
5. a
6. k
7. i
8. c
9. g
10. b
11. true
12. true
13. false
14. true
15. false
16. false
17. false
18. true
19. true
20. false
21. Any order:
a. prophet
b. priest
c. judge
22. a. Saul
b. David
c. Solomon
23. a. Job
b. Psalms
c. Proverbs
d. Ecclesiastes
e. Song of Solomon
24. Any order:
a. Solomon
b. Agur
c. Lemuel
25. b
26. a
27. b
28. c
29. d
30. They told Job he must have sinned and his suffering was punishment from God.
31. Imprecatory Psalms invoke a curse or judgement upon an enemy of God and man.

BIBLE 1006

ALTERNATE LIFEPAC TEST

NAME ______________________

DATE ______________________

SCORE ______________________

Match these items (each answer, 2 points).

1. ________ David
2. ________ Merab
3. ________ Bath-sheba
4. ________ Hiram
5. ________ theocracy
6. ________ dialectic
7. ________ Adonijah
8. ________ Saul
9. ________ Nathan
10. ________ shophetim

a. God reigning as king
b. judgeship
c. a Benjamite
d. David's brother
e. from the tribe of Judah
f. Saul's daughter
g. a prophet
h. one of David's wives
i. David's eldest son
j. king of Tyre
k. dialogue

Write true or false (each answer, 1 point).

11. ____________ The books of First and Second Samuel were originally written as one book.
12. ____________ A line of faithful priests extended from Samuel to Christ.
13. ____________ Saul patiently waited for Samuel at Gilgal.
14. ____________ David's first responsibility as king was to establish a capital city.
15. ____________ Amasa was slain by Absalom.
16. ____________ Solomon never offered sacrifices to the Lord.
17. ____________ Solomon's wisdom was demonstrated when he cut a child in half.

18. ____________ Solomon prayed the longest prayer found in the Bible.

19. ____________ Elihu told Job that Job's suffering had been for good.

20. ____________ The book of Psalms is divided into seven separate books of Psalms in the Hebrew text.

Complete these lists (each answer, 3 points).

21. List the three offices of Samuel.

a. ____________________ b. ____________________ c. ____________________

22. List in order the first three kings of Israel.

a. ____________________ b. ____________________ c. ____________________

23. List in order the five books of Hebrew poetry found in the Scriptures.

a. ____________________ b. ____________________ c. ____________________

d. ____________________ e. ____________________

24. List the three writers of the Proverbs.

a. ____________________ b. ____________________ c. ____________________

Write the letter for the correct answer on each line (each answer, 2 points).

25. Hebrew poetry is characterized by ____________ .

a. prophecy b. parallelism c. free verse d. history

26. Hebrew poetry that repeats in similar words a previous line is ________________ .

a. synonymous b. antithetic c. synthetic d. climactic

27. Hebrew poetry that contrasts ideas is ________________ .

a. synonymous b. antithetic c. synthetic d. climactic

28. When something is added to a second line of Hebrew poetry, it is called ________________ .

a. synonymous b. antithetic c. synthetic d. climactic

29. Poetry that builds to a crescendo of concept is ________________ .

a. synonymous b. antithetic c. synthetic d. climactic

Complete these activities (each answer, 5 points).

30. Describe the reason for Job's suffering as explained by his three comforters.

____

____

____

31. Describe the purpose of the Imprecatory Psalms.

____

____

____

BIBLE 1007

Unit 7: The Divided Kingdom

TEACHER NOTES

MATERIALS NEEDED FOR LIFEPAC	
Required	Suggested
• none	• Bible, King James Version • other versions of the Bible if permitted • wall map of the Land of Israel during the period of the divided kingdom • Unger's or Halley's Bible handbook • Bible atlas • Bible dictionary • Bible concordance • paperback edition of Roget's thesaurus • the reference materials can be in either book or online formats

ADDITIONAL LEARNING ACTIVITIES

Section 1: From Jeroboam to Ahab

1. Using the errors of both Jeroboam and Rehoboam as examples, discuss how the plan of God continues regardless of the sins of men. Seek to show that God's plan is not subject to human frailties.
2. Using the division of the kingdom and the subsequent sins of the kings of Israel and Judah, discuss the value of integrity and a right heart on the part of those who serve the Lord God.
3. Have a group of students make two corresponding time lines that illustrate the kings and the activities of the Northern and Southern Kingdoms during the period covered in this section of the LIFEPAC.
4. Divide the students into two teams and have the teams debate to which kingdom they would have wished to belong. Subsequent history should be used; however, only the information available at the beginning of these kingdoms can be introduced as evidence.
5. Make two charts for classroom display listing the kings of Israel and Judah. Identify each king in the correct order, and list the dates of his reign.
6. Using additional sources, write a two-page report on the Samaritans. Show their history up to the time of Christ.
7. Students may write a 500-word report on Jeroboam and Rehoboam. Additional sources are to be used as the student compares the characters of the two kings.

Section 2: From Ahab to Jehu

1. A game can be played that would involve the entire class in identifying the kings of Israel and Judah. Take a single event or description of one king and write it on one side of an index card, with the name of the king on the other side. Draw one card at a time, read the

description, and see if the students can name the king. Teams can be selected to compete against each other.

2. Discuss how God allowed His people to go after strange gods but would not bless them during their course of sin. Seek to show the compassion and loving kindness of God toward His people in this discussion.
3. Have groups of students produce skits that illustrate any of the events discussed in the first and second section of this LIFEPAC.
4. Have the students make posters and charts that compare and contrast the character and ministries of Elijah and Elisha.
5. Make a chart that illustrates the differences in content of 2 Kings and 2 Chronicles.
6. Using additional sources, write a report on one of the kings of Judah discussed in this section of the LIFEPAC.

Section 3: From Jehu to the Assyrian Captivity

1. Discuss the extreme actions of Jehu, who was commissioned by God to rid Israel of evil. Show how God may for a time tolerate evil on the part of His people, but judgment is always sure to come. Compare those times with our present day and circumstances. Or write a report explaining whether or not you feel Jehu was justified in his actions.
2. Discuss and compare the cycles of divine discipline revealed in Leviticus 26:14–39 with the disasters that plagued Israel as they were judged by God for their evil errors. See if the cycles are demonstrated in the fall of the Northern Kingdom.
3. Have the students discuss and debate what action should have been taken by the leaders of Israel as they found themselves under domination by the Assyrians. Should they have continued to pay the tribute? Should an alliance with Egypt have been sought? What help could they have received from Judah? Who was the source of their only real hope?
4. Have the students make a time line and a display of posters that will portray the history of the Assyrian Empire.
5. Using additional sources, write a report on Athaliah and her evil activities.

Section 4: The Prophets of the Period

1. Discuss the ministry, duties, and responsibilities of the prophets of the Old Testament. Explain that these prophets were as much forth tellers as fore tellers.
2. Play a game that will help the students identify the prophets of this period. On one side of an index card list a verse, event, or description of one of the prophets and, on the other side, the name of the prophet. Read the verse, event, or description to the class and have the students identify the prophet.
3. Have a spelling bee using the names of the kings of Israel and Judah as the vocabulary.
4. Have the students make various charts or posters illustrating the contents of the books written by the prophets of this period.
5. Have the students act out the book of Jonah. Have the students write a script, select the players, and present the skit to the class.
6. Make a time line showing the times of the ministries of the prophets during this period of Old Testament history.

STUDENT WORKSHEETS

The activity on the following page may be reproduced as a student worksheet.

» ANSWER KEY

1. KJ
2. KI
3. KI
4. KI
5. KJ
6. KI
7. KI
8. KI
9. KJ
10. P
11. P
12. KJ
13. KI
14. P
15. KJ
16. P
17. P
18. KJ
19. KI
20. KI
21. KJ

Administer the LIFEPAC Test.
The test is to be administered in one session. Give no help except with directions.
Evaluate the tests and review areas where the students have done poorly.
Review the pages and activities that stress the concepts tested.
If necessary, administer the Alternate LIFEPAC Test.

» KINGS, KINGS, AND PROPHETS

In this LIFEPAC you have studied the kings of Israel, some of the kings of Judah, and the early prophets of the Old Testament period. The following list is of some of the people you studied in this LIFEPAC. Identify them by marking them either as a king of Israel (KI), a king of Judah (KJ), or as a prophet (P).

1. ______________ Rehoboam
2. ______________ Omri
3. ______________ Jeroboam
4. ______________ Jehu
5. ______________ Abijah
6. ______________ Zimri
7. ______________ Shallum
8. ______________ Pekah
9. ______________ Asa
10. ______________ Joel
11. ______________ Jonah
12. ______________ Jehoshaphat
13. ______________ Baasha
14. ______________ Elijah
15. ______________ Joash
16. ______________ Obadiah
17. ______________ Hosea
18. ______________ Amaziah
19. ______________ Nadab
20. ______________ Ahab
21. ______________ Hezekiah

ANSWER KEYS

SECTION 1

1.1 a. Saul
b. David
c. Solomon
d. Rehoboam
e. Jeroboam

1.2 Either order:
a. Solomon
b. Rehoboam

1.3 alleviate the oppressive measures instituted by Solomon

1.4 more oppressive measures

1.5 a. against Rehoboam
b. Jeroboam king

1.6 Either order:
a. that ten tribes would be torn from the hand of Solomon's son and given to Jeroboam
b. that his house would be established in Israel like the house of David

1.7 Either order:
a. he must keep God's commandments
b. he must walk in God's ways

1.8 unbelief

1.9 a. two golden calves
b. them to be Israel's gods

1.10 Either order:
a. Bethel
b. Dan

1.11 Levites

1.12 a. feasts that he had instituted
b. sacrifices upon altars that he had established

1.13 a. Judah
b. Bethel

1.14 a. Josiah
b. altar at Bethel

1.15 a. altar
b. ashes

1.16 a. withering
b. hand
c. prayer

1.17 repent

1.18 Either order:
a. Jeroboam
b. Israel

1.19 a. son
b. house

1.20 a. displaced
b. land
c. Assyrian Captivity

1.21 a. Rehoboam
b. Abijah
c. Asa

1.22 He forsook the Law of the Lord (2 Chronicles 12:1).

1.23 with Judah

1.24 Example:
All the golden treasures of the Temple that Solomon had made, including the shields of gold, were taken by Shishak, king of Egypt, and were replaced with brazen shields by Rehoboam.

1.25 because they relied upon the Lord

1.26 for forty-one years

1.27 his stern and aggressive attack upon immorality and idolatry

1.28 Jeroboam and Ahab

1.29 because they recognized that God was with Judah

1.30 Example:
because he appealed to Ben-hadad of Syria for assistance against Israel, sending him silver and gold out of the treasures of the Temple

1.31 c

1.32 c

1.33 b

1.34 d

1.35 c

1.36 b

1.37 a

1.38 b

1.39 a

1.40 d

SELF TEST 1

1.01 false
1.02 false
1.03 true
1.04 true
1.05 false
1.06 Ahab
1.07 Baasha
1.08 a. Asa
b. Judah
1.09 a. Asa's
b. Judah
1.010 Rehoboam's
1.011 Jeroboam
1.012 a. Jeroboam
b. withering
1.013 c
1.014 e
1.015 b
1.016 a
1.017 d
1.018 Example:
In the midst of wisdom, wealth, and honor from God, Solomon had sinned. His home was turned into a harem, his wives turned his heart after their gods, and the city of the Lord was corrupted by high places for the worship of false gods.
1.019 Example:
Asa was rebuked of the Lord through Hanani the seer because he relied upon Ben-hadad of Syria for assistance against Israel.
1.020 Example:
All the golden treasures of the Temple that Solomon had made, including the shields of gold, were taken by Shishak, king of Egypt, and were replaced with brazen shields by Rehoboam.
1.021 because they relied upon the Lord
1.022 God used Baasha to destroy the house of Jeroboam because of Jeroboam's sin.

SECTION 2

2.1 false
2.2 true
2.3 true
2.4 true
2.5 false
2.6 true
2.7 false
2.8 false
2.9 true
2.10 true
2.11 a. go show himself to Ahab
b. send rain upon the earth
2.12 a. everywhere
b. trouble
2.13 a. trouble
b. forsaken the commandments of the LORD, and followed Baalim
2.14 a. 450
b. 400
2.15 a. morning
b. noon
c. evening
2.16 The altar of the Lord (that was broken down)
2.17 a. twelve
b. water
c. poured
2.18 Either order:
a. to assure that no fire had been placed under the wood and sacrifice
b. to demonstrate faith in God for the water they would need
2.19 a. Abraham
b. Isaac
c. Israel
2.20 The LORD, he is the God; the LORD, he is the God.
2.21 the rain stop him
2.22 Jezebel warned Elijah that he would be dead within twenty-four hours.
2.23 Example:
Approaching Horeb, Elijah felt alone in his stand for God in Israel.
2.24 Example:
Departing Horeb, Elijah was reassured by God that he was not alone in Israel; but, rather, he was among seven thousand others who had not bowed their knees to Baal.
2.25 Elijah was assigned by God to anoint (answer in any order):
1) Elisha as his successor,
2) Hazael to be king over Syria, and
3) Jehu to be king over Israel.

2.26 Elijah personally anointed Elisha to be his successor.
2.27 He was LORD
2.28 the Law of Moses
2.29 Micaiah
2.30 Elijah's
2.31 a. Jehoshaphat
b. Ahab
2.32 a. good
b. evil
2.33 God
2.34 sending priests and teachers throughout Judah to teach the Law of the Lord
2.35 a. Israel
b. divided
2.36 Any order:
a. a military alliance with Ahab against Syria
b. an economic alliance with Ahaziah involving ships
c. a matrimonial alliance—Jehoshaphat's son married Ahab's and Jezebel's daughter
2.37 Either order:
a. father (Ahab)
b. mother (Jezebel)
2.38 fall
2.39 a. The city of Ekron
b. god
c. Ekron
d. recover
2.40 Elijah
2.41 a. consumed
b. fire
c. heaven
2.42 a. Elijah
b. died
c. word of the Lord
2.43 true
2.44 true
2.45 false
2.46 true
2.47 false
2.48 true
2.49 true
2.50 true
2.51 brother
2.52 a. Jehoshaphat
b. Edom
2.53 water
2.54 sought
2.55 a. water
b. deliver the Moabites into their hands
2.56 Either order:
a. wind
b. rain
2.57 a. eldest son
b. burnt sacrifice
2.58 a. left the scene of battle
b. returned to their own lands
2.59 Example:
The widow of a student prophet was in debt and distress. Her creditor was about to take her two sons as slaves.
2.60 Example:
Elisha instructed the widow to borrow several vessels from her neighbors, and her oil was miraculously increased to fill the vessels. She had enough to sell and pay her debts and live on the rest.
2.61 The Shunammite woman was given a son.
2.62 The son died, and he was brought back to life to his mother in response to her faith.
2.63 Examples (either order):
a. The student prophets had unknowingly added poisonous gourds to their herb soup, and Elisha told them to add some meal. The soup was made edible by the power of God through Elisha.
b. Elisha was given twenty loaves of barley bread, and he shared that bread with one hundred people, with bread to spare.
2.64 a. Lord
b. leper
2.65 a. maid
b. king
2.66 Elisha
2.67 seven times
2.68 a. faith
b. God
2.69 leper
2.70 a. king
b. Lord
c. Elisha
2.71 horses and chariots of fire
2.72 Elisha
2.73 Any order:
a. chariots
b. horses
c. a great host
2.74 camp
2.75 lepers
2.76 a. twenty-four
b. Elisha

2.77 a. Hazael
b. throne.
2.78 a. Damascus
b. Hazael
c. Ben-hadad
2.79 Jehoshaphat
2.80 killing all six of his brothers
2.81 a. Athaliah
b. Ahab
c. Jezebel
2.82 father-in-law (Ahab)
2.83 politically
2.84 youngest
2.85 mother
2.86 Jehu

SELF TEST 2

2.01 c
2.02 a
2.03 a
2.04 d
2.05 c
2.06 true
2.07 false
2.08 false
2.09 false
2.010 true
2.011 a. gourds
b. bread
2.012 a. Jehoram
b. Jehoshaphat
2.013 his mother
2.014 Jehu
2.015 Elijah
2.016 Baal
2.017 Jehoshaphat
2.018 the spirit of Elijah
2.019 Example:
Jehoram walked not in the ways of his father (Jehoshaphat), but in the ways of his father-in-law (Ahab) He did not walk righteously, but unrighteously.
2.020 Example:
The young people's words, "Go up, thou bald head," probably referred to the translation by the Lord of Elijah (by the words "go up"), whom the followers of Baal held in contempt; and the nickname "bald head" was a disrespectful attack attributing dishonor or disgrace to the man of God and, therefore, to God Himself.
2.021 Jezebel warned Elijah that he would be dead within twenty-four hours.
2.022 "The LORD, he is the God; the LORD, he is the God."
2.023 Hint:
Answer should contain the basic ideas of 1 Kings 18:18: "I have not troubled Israel; but thou, and thy father's house, in that ye have forsaken the commandments of the LORD, and thou hast followed Baalim."

SECTION 3

3.1 d
3.2 b
3.3 a
3.4 a
3.5 b
3.6 a
3.7 b
3.8 d
3.9 e
3.10 f
3.11 c
3.12 b
3.13 c
3.14 e
3.15 e
3.16 c
3.17 a
3.18 d
3.19 d
3.20 d
3.21 Judah
3.22 52
3.23 pride
3.24 a. priests
b. incense
c. incense
3.25 a. priestly
b. leprosy
3.26 Any order:
a. silver
b. wheat
c. barley
3.27 Jehu
3.28 a. Shallum
b. one
3.29 Ahaz
3.30 Hoshea

SELF TEST 3

3.01 false
3.02 true
3.03 true
3.04 false
3.05 true
3.06 c
3.07 f *or* b
3.08 a
3.09 d
3.010 e
3.011 Naaman
3.012 Ahaziah
3.013 Jehu
3.014 a. priests
b. altars
c. broken down
3.015 Joash
3.016 Azariah
3.017 Zechariah
3.018 Hoshea
3.019 Example:
The ancestors of the Samaritans of Jesus' day were other people conquered by Tiglathpileser and relocated in Samaria after the Assyrian Captivity of Israel.
3.020 In Joash, the line of David was preserved.
3.021 Jehu was commissioned by the Lord to destroy the worshipers of Baal in Israel.
3.022 Example:
Athaliah wickedly influenced the reigns in Judah of her husband Jehoram and her son Ahaziah. She introduced Baal worship in Judah. For six years, she reigned a wicked reign in Jerusalem, usurping the throne of David.
3.023 "The LORD, he is the God; the LORD, he is the God."

SECTION 4

4.1 Either order:
a. south
b. east

4.2 Either order:
a. Philistines
b. Arabians

4.3 servant of Jehovah

4.4 shortest

4.5 a. I. THE ANNOUNCEMENT OF JUDGMENT 1:1-9
b. II. THE REASONS FOR JUDGMENT 1:10-16
c. III. THE RESTITUTION OF JUDAH 1:17-21

4.6 Obadiah

4.7 a. Judah
b. Jerusalem

4.8 Temple

4.9 priests

4.10 a. Joash
b. Jehoiada

4.11 The Day of the Lord

4.12 Either order (a, b):
a. literal historical
b. predicted endtime
c. both

4.13 Jehovah is my God

4.14 a. outpouring of the Holy Spirit
b. Day of Pentecost
c. Peter
d. Acts 2:16–21

4.15 a. Jeroboam (II)
b. Israel
c. 2 Kings 14:25

4.16 Nineveh

4.17 a. Tarshish
b. opposite

4.18 repentance

4.19 a. Christ
b. Matthew 12:39–41 or Luke 11:29–32

4.20 a. I. JONAH'S CALL AND DISOBEDIENCE chapter 1
b. II. JONAH'S PRAYER AND DELIVERANCE chapter 2
c. III. JONAH'S PREACHING AND NINEVEH'S REPENTANCE chapter 3
d. IV. JONAH'S DISCOURAGEMENT AND GOD'S INSTRUCTION chapter 4

4.21 a. Judah
b. Israel

4.22 a. repent
b. repentance
c. righteousness

4.23 predicted

4.24 a. captivity
b. Damascus
c. Assyrian Captivity

4.25 a. utterly destroy the house of Jacob
b. raise up the tabernacle of David
c. Lord Jesus Christ

4.26 Northern

4.27 one half of a century or 50 years

4.28 a. Jeroboam (II)
b. Hezekiah

4.29 divine love

4.30 a. Gomer
b. God's
c. Israel

SELF TEST 4

4.01 5
4.02 4
4.03 8
4.04 10
4.05 3
4.06 1
4.07 9
4.08 6
4.09 2
4.010 7
4.011 a. Obadiah
b. Jerusalem
4.012 Joel
4.013 Jonah
4.014 Hosea
4.015 a. Amos
b. Israel
4.016 Jonah
4.017 Judah
4.018 Hosea
4.019 God's love for Israel
4.020 Either order:
a. that the house of Jacob would not utterly be destroyed
b. that the tabernacle of David would be raised up
4.021 In Joash, the line of David was preserved.
4.022 Hint:
Answer should contain the basic ideas of 1 Kings 18:18: "I have not troubled Israel; but thou, and thy father's house, in that ye have forsaken the commandments of the LORD, and thou hast followed Baalim."
4.023 Example:
Asa was rebuked of the Lord through Hanani the seer because he relied upon Ben-hadad of Syria for assistance against Israel.

LIFEPAC TEST

1. c
2. d
3. e
4. d
5. c
6. true
7. true
8. true
9. false
10. false
11. Bethel
12. Nadab
13. Jehu
14. Asa's
15. forsaking the Law of the Lord
16. withholding of the rain
17. confessed faith in the God of Israel
18. a. Jehoshaphat
b. Law of the Lord
19. Carmel
20. 4
21. 9
22. 7
23. 2
24. 5
25. 6
26. 1
27. 10
28. 3
29. 8
30. Example:
Athaliah wickedly influenced the reigns in Judah of her husband Jehoram and her son Ahaziah. She introduced Baal worship in Judah. For six years, she reigned a wicked reign in Jerusalem, usurping the throne of David.
31. Example:
In the midst of wisdom, wealth, and honor from God, Solomon had sinned. His home was turned into a harem, his wives turned his heart away after their gods, and the city of the Lord was corrupted by high places for the worship of false gods.

ALTERNATE LIFEPAC TEST

1. b
2. g
3. d
4. k
5. f
6. h
7. c
8. i
9. e
10. a
11. true
12. false
13. true
14. false
15. false
16. true
17. true
18. true
19. false
20. false
21. unbelief
22. Dan
23. Israel
24. Jehoshaphat
25. Elisha
26. Athaliah
27. Judah
28. Joash
29. 2
30. 1
31. 7
32. 3
33. 6
34. 8
35. 9
36. 4
37. 10
38. 5
39. 13
40. 17
41. 19
42. 14
43. 12
44. 18
45. 15
46. 11
47. 16
48. Any order:
    a. his son would die
    b. his dynasty would be destroyed
    c. Israel would be displaced
49. Any order:
    a. Obadiah
    b. Joel
    c. Jonah
    d. Amos
    e. Hosea
50. Either order:
    a. not to utterly destroy the house of Jacob
    b. raise up the tabernacle of David

BIBLE 1007

ALTERNATE LIFEPAC TEST

NAME ____________________

DATE ____________________

SCORE ____________________

Match these items (each answer, 2 points).

1. ________ Jeroboam
2. ________ Micaiah
3. ________ Judah
4. ________ Tiglath-Pileser
5. ________ Ben-hadad
6. ________ Naaman
7. ________ Josiah
8. ________ Athaliah
9. ________ Israel
10. ________ Rehoboam

a. Solomon's son
b. promised a *sure house*
c. would destroy the altars of Bethel
d. Southern Kingdom
e. Northern Kingdom
f. king of Syria
g. a prophet
h. a leper
i. daughter of Jezebel
j. son of Asa
k. repopulated Samaria

Write true or false (each answer, 1 point).

11. ____________ Jeraboam was told to keep God's commandments and walk in God's way.
12. ____________ Rehoboam followed the poor advice of the elders.
13. ____________ Rehoboam's son was Abijah.
14. ____________ Asa reigned in Israel for forty-one years.
15. ____________ Jehoram was the father of Jehoshaphat.
16. ____________ Joash reigned prior to Ahaziah.
17. ____________ Azariah reigned in Judah for fifty-two years.

18. ____________ Jehu was appointed by God to destroy the house of Ahab.

19. ____________ Second Kings relates the dynasty of Saul.

20. ____________ Jehu's house ruled over Judah for four generations.

Complete these statements (each answer, 3 points).

21. Jeroboam's first sin as king was the sin of ____________________ .

22. Jerobaom placed pagan altars in the cities of Bethel and ____________________ .

23. Elijah's ministry concentrated on the nation of ____________________ .

24. The Moabites and the Ammonites invaded Judah during the reign of ____________________ .

25. Elijah's ministry was followed by the ministry of ____________________ .

26. The mother of Ahaziah was ____________________ .

27. Chronicles deals exclusively with the nation of ____________________ .

28. In Israel the line of David was preserved in ____________________ .

Indicate the correct chronological order for these two groups of kings of Israel by placing numbers on the lines from 1 to 10 in the first column and 11 to 19 in the second column, beginning with the earliest king in each group (each answer, 2 points).

29. ____________ Nadab

30. ____________ Jeroboam

31. ____________ Ahab

32. ____________ Baasha

33. ____________ Omri

34. ____________ Ahaziah

35. ____________ Joram

36. ____________ Elah

37. ____________ Jehu

38. ____________ Zimri

39. ____________ Jeroboam II

40. ____________ Pekahiah

41. ____________ Hoshea

42. ____________ Zechariah

43. ____________ Jehoash

44. ____________ Pekah

45. ____________ Shallum

46. ____________ Jehoahaz

47. ____________ Menahem

Complete these activities (each answer, 3 points).

48. List the three judgments pronounced by Abijah upon Jeroboam.

a. ______________________________

b. ______________________________

c. ______________________________

49. List the prophets of the period studied in this LIFEPAC.

a. ____________________

b. ____________________

c. ____________________

d. ____________________

e. ____________________

50. List the two promises made by Amos to Israel.

a. ______________________________

b. ______________________________

BIBLE 1008

Unit 8: The Remaining Kingdom

TEACHER NOTES

MATERIALS NEEDED FOR LIFEPAC	
Required	Suggested
• none	• Bible, King James Version • other versions of the Bible if permitted • wall map of the Land of Israel showing the kingdoms of Israel, Judah, Assyria, and Babylon • Unger's or Halley's Bible handbook • Bible atlas • Bible dictionary • Bible concordance • paperback edition of Roget's thesaurus • *International Standard Bible Encyclopedia* or *Zondervan Pictorial Encyclopedia of the Bible* • the reference materials can be in either book or online formats

ADDITIONAL LEARNING ACTIVITIES

Section 1: Hezekiah

1. Using the revival and reform of Hezekiah as an illustration, discuss the need for such action today. We have seen revival in past centuries, but is there such movement of the Spirit today? Discuss what would happen if the United States experienced such revival during the latter part of this century.
2. Discuss how God chose to use the heathen nation of Assyria to discipline His people. Would God, in contemporary times, use the unbeliever to correct the errors of the people of God?
3. Have the students make a time line that shows the events of the Assyrian Empire during the period covered in this LIFEPAC. Begin with the fall of Israel and end with the Babylonian conquest of Assyria, about 612 B.C. This could be a group or individual project.
4. Have a group of students produce a skit that will illustrate any of the important events in the life of Hezekiah.
5. Select, practice, and present an oral reading of any portion of Scripture that deals with the life of Hezekiah.
6. Make a time line showing the important events and actions of Hezekiah as he reigned over Judah

Section 2: From Manasseh to Josiah

1. Using the reign of Manasseh as an illustration, discuss the character of apostasy and idolatry. Seek to have the students realize that an idol is anything that man regards as more important than the Lord.

2. Using the discovery of the written Law during the reign of Josiah, discuss the importance of a daily Bible study for the Christian.
3. Have the students make a time line that shows the chronological order of the events discussed in this section of the LIFEPAC.
4. Have a group of students present a skit portraying the rediscovery of the written Law during Josiah's reign.
5. Using additional sources, write a report on either Manasseh, Amon, or Josiah. Make sure the information used is found in sources other than your LIFEPAC.
6. Using the style of an eyewitness reporter for the *Jerusalem Gazette*, write a paper chronicling the reforms of Josiah.

Section 3: From Jehoahaz to Exile

1. Divide the class into teams. Read off events that happened during the reign of Judah, and have the teams guess which king is associated with the event. Extra credit points could be awarded to the team with the most correct answers.
2. Compare the fall of Israel and the fall of Judah. Consider the reasons for the judgment and the similarities of the captivities.
3. Have the students discuss and debate what they would do if they were living in Jerusalem at the time of its fall. Would they surrender to the Babylonians, remain and fight to the death, or try to escape the onslaught?
4. Have the students research and make charts or posters that show how God's promise to David continued through the fall of Judah and eventually was realized in the Lord Jesus Christ.
5. Using sources other than your LIFEPAC, write a paper on Nebuchadnezzar, the king of Babylon.
6. Make a time line showing the fall of Judah. Begin with the reign of Josiah and end with the fall of the Holy City, Jerusalem.
7. The student may write a 500-word report on the rise of the Babylonian Empire. Sources other than this LIFEPAC should be used to complete this paper.

Section 4: The Prophets of the Period

1. Have the students compare the ministries of Isaiah and Jeremiah. Show how both men ministered to God's people during times of crisis. Discuss the people's attitude to the messengers of the Lord. Show how God always provides His Word during trials.
2. Have a spelling bee using the names of the kings and prophets as vocabulary words.
3. Read selected verses from the books of the prophets and see if the students can identify the author. The class could be divided into teams, and the winners may receive extra points.
4. Have the students make time lines and posters depicting the duration of each prophet mentioned in this section of the LIFEPAC.
5. Have the students make posters illustrating the books written by the prophets.
6. Select, practice, and present an oral reading from one of the books of the prophets of this period. Include background information about the prophet and his message.
7. Write a report on one of the prophets discussed in this LIFEPAC. Use information not found in this LIFEPAC.

STUDENT WORKSHEET

The activity on the following page may be reproduced as a student worksheet.

» ANSWER KEY

1. Obadiah
2. Joel
3. Jonah
4. Hosea
5. Amos
6. Isaiah
7. Micah
8. Nahum
9. Zephaniah
10. Jeremiah
11. Habakkuk

Theme: Any reasonable answer is acceptable.

Question: Any reasonable answer is acceptable.

Administer the LIFEPAC Test.
The test is to be administered in one session. Give no help except with directions.
Evaluate the tests and review areas where the students have done poorly.
Review the pages and activities that stress the concepts tested.
If necessary, administer the Alternate LIFEPAC Test.

» THE PROPHETS OF JUDAH AND ISRAEL

In this LIFEPAC you have studied six of the prophets that ministered during the time of the divided kingdom. In the previous LIFEPAC you studied five prophets of this divided period. The following list contains the prophets of Israel and Judah. Arrange them in chronological order on the center lines and then write the general theme of their message on the lines in the column to the right.

		PROPHET	THEME
Habakkuk	1.	____________	______________________________
Nahum	2.	____________	______________________________
Obadiah	3.	____________	______________________________
Hosea	4.	____________	______________________________
Joel	5.	____________	______________________________
Zephaniah	6.	____________	______________________________
Isaiah	7.	____________	______________________________
Jonah	8.	____________	______________________________
Micah	9.	____________	______________________________
Amos	10.	____________	______________________________
Jeremiah	11.	____________	______________________________

Answer this question: If you could only have a single copy of the message of one of the listed prophets, which one would you select? Explain your answer.

____

____

____

____

____

____

ANSWER KEYS

SECTION 1

1.1 Ahaz
1.2 2 Kings 18:12
1.3 a. space
b. Bible
1.4 Any order:
a. 2 Kings 18-20
b. 2 Chronicles 29-32
c. Isaiah 36-39
1.5 a. Asa
b. third
1.6 David
1.7 return to the Lord
1.8 Ahaz
1.9 Either order:
a. opening
b. repairing
1.10 a. sanctify
b. cleanse
1.11 a. cleansed
b. cleansed or sanctified
1.12 a. divine prescription
b. Law of Moses
1.13 sang praises
1.14 a. bowed
b. worshiped
1.15 Israel
1.16 Either order (b, c):
a. Passover
b. Israel
c. Judah
1.17 first
1.18 second
1.19 Either order:
a. Levitical defilement
b. absence
1.20 Passover
1.21 life
1.22 a. idols
b. groves
c. high places
1.23 b
1.24 b
1.25 c
1.26 b
1.27 d
1.28 a. the house of the Lord
b. Isaiah
1.29 Example:
In response to the letter he received from Sennacherib, Hezekiah went to the house of the Lord, spread the letter out before the Lord, and prayed.
1.30 Example:
Hezekiah asked the Lord to save Judah that all the world might know that He and only He was God.
1.31 false
1.32 false
1.33 false
1.34 true
1.35 a. gifts
b. Jerusalem
1.36 twenty-five
1.37 fourteenth
1.38 thirty-nine
1.39 a. prayer
b. tears
c. heal thee
1.40 a. three
b. fifteen
1.41 a. stopped
b. reversed
1.42 a. ambassadors
b. king
c. Babylon
1.43 a. gloried
b. grace
1.44 first prophecy of the Babylonian Captivity

SELF TEST 1

1.01 false
1.02 true
1.03 true
1.04 false
1.05 false
1.06 d
1.07 d
1.08 b
1.09 c
1.010 a
1.011 Either order:
a. Levitical defilement
b. absence
1.012 Nehushtan
1.013 a. idol
b. incense
c. burned
1.014 Sennacherib
1.015 Babylon
1.016 a. folly or sin of pride
b. Babylonian Captivity
1.017 Example:
God's sign to Hezekiah confirming this promise involved a miracle in which the earth was probably stopped in its rotation movement and actually reversed.
1.018 Example:
Hezekiah asked the Lord to save Judah that all the world might know that He and only He was God.
1.019 Example:
In response to the letter he received from Sennacherib, Hezekiah went to the house of the Lord, spread the letter out before the Lord, and prayed.
1.020 Example:
Hezekiah was probably about thirty-nine years of age when his message of death came from the Lord by Isaiah. He was twenty-five years old when he began to reign in Judah; and in the fourteenth year of his reign, God had delivered Judah from Sennacherib. This was only shortly before his sickness.
1.021 Example:
The king's commandments and the priests' responses were according to the divine prescription of the Law of Moses.

SECTION 2

2.1 twelve
2.2 Hezekiah
2.3 Any order:
a. He built again the high places.
b. He built altars for Baal.
c. He made groves.
d. He built idolatrous altars in the house of the Lord.
or offered his children as sacrifices, practiced witchcraft and spiritism, placed carved image in the house of the Lord.
2.4 the house of the Lord
2.5 a. heathen
b. destroyed
c. Canaan
2.6 would not listen
2.7 a. Assyrian
b. Babylon
2.8 Either order (b, c):
a. Lord
b. humility
c. prayer
2.9 He was God
2.10 Any order:
a. He removed the idol from the house of the Lord.
b. He cast out of Jerusalem all the altars of false worship.
c. The altar of the Lord was repaired.
d. The Levitical sacrifices were re-established.
2.11 Amon was twenty–two years old when he began to reign in Jerusalem, and he reigned two years.
2.12 Example:
Amon humbled not himself before the Lord as Manasseh, his father, had humbled himself; but Amon trespassed more and more–multiplying guilt.
2.13 a. Asa
b. Hezekiah
c. Josiah
2.14 sixteen
2.15 twelfth
2.16 a. priests
b. altars
2.17 e
2.18 c
2.19 a
2.20 b

2.21 Example:
In 1 Kings 13:2 is recorded the prophesy of the birth of Josiah and against the altar in Bethel, which Josiah destroyed in fulfillment of that prophesy.

2.22 Example:
The reforms of Josiah were so thorough that all the idolatrous abominations were removed from all the territory that belonged to the children of Israel, and everyone served the Lord.

2.23 Example:
The Lord turned not from the fierceness of His anger kindled against Judah, and He confirmed His word concerning the captivity of Judah that would occur (2 Kings 21:14; 23:26-27).

SELF TEST 2

2.01 true
2.02 false
2.03 false
2.04 false
2.05 false
2.06 Canaanites
2.07 Hezekiah
2.08 Josiah
2.09 Amon
2.010 Israel
2.011 eighth
2.012 Passover
2.013 Law of Moses
2.014 keep His commandments
2.015 Hezekiah
2.016 d
2.017 e
2.018 b
2.019 c
2.020 f
2.021 Example:
The reforms of Josiah were so thorough that all the idolatrous abominations were removed from all the territory that belonged to the children of Israel, and everyone served the Lord.

2.022 Example:
Amon had not humbled himself before the Lord, as Manasseh his father had humbled himself; but Amon trespassed more and more—multiplying guilt.

2.023 Example:
2 Kings 13:2 recorded the prophesy of the birth of Josiah and against the altar in Bethel, which Josiah destroyed in fulfillment of that prophesy.

2.024 Example:
God's sign to Hezekiah confirming His promise involved a miracle in which the earth was probably stopped in its rotation and actually reversed.

2.025 Hezekiah asked the Lord to save Judah that all the world might know that He and only He was God.

SECTION 3

3.1 c
3.2 a
3.3 b
3.4 a
3.5 d
3.6 d
3.7 c
3.8 b
3.9 b
3.10 a
3.11 Example:
Apparently, Jehoiakim was made Nebuchadnezzar's servant and either left in Jerusalem (a change of mind on the part of Nebuchadnezzar) or later returned to Jerusalem (see 2 Kings 24:6 and Jeremiah 22:18-19).
3.12 Daniel
3.13 a. Jeremiah
b. righteousness
3.14 a. Jeremiah
b. Babylonian Captivity
c. burning
3.15 a. end of his house
b. death
3.16 a. Evil-merodach
b. Nebuchadnezzar
3.17 Jehoiachin was allowed to eat at the royal table, and he was given an allowance to support his servants and attendants.
3.18 ninth
3.19 a. eleventh
b. one
c. six
3.20 Southern Kingdom
3.21 true
3.22 false
3.23 true
3.24 true
3.25 true

SELF TEST 3

3.01 false
3.02 true
3.03 true
3.04 true
3.05 false
3.06 c
3.07 a
3.08 d
3.09 c
3.010 b
3.011 Carchemish
3.012 Jehoiakim
3.013 thirty-six
3.014 Zedekiah
3.015 David
3.016 conditional
3.017 history of redemption
3.018 promise of God
3.019 two and one-half
3.020 Zedekiah
3.021 Example:
The Lord turned not from the fierceness of His anger kindled against Judah, and He confirmed His word concerning the captivity of Judah that would occur (2 Kings 21:14; 23:26-27).
3.022 Example:
Daniel 1:1 probably refers to the departure of Nebuchadnezzar from Babylon for Jerusalem, and Jeremiah 46:2 probably refers to the actual arrival of Nebuchadnezzar in Jerusalem. Also, Nebuchadnezzar was probably only a representative of his father, Nabopolassur, when he went first to Jerusalem; and he did not likely become king in Babylon until the death of his father—about two years after his first departure from Babylon for Jerusalem.
3.023 Example:
Jehoiakim burned the book (scroll) containing God's final message to him by Jeremiah because it predicted the Babylonian Captivity.
3.024 to walk before God in truth with all their hearts and with all their souls
3.025 Example:
God's promise to David by Nathan the prophet concerning an everlasting kingdom was an unconditional promise that would be fulfilled in Christ.

SECTION 4

4.1 Amos
4.2 prominence
4.3 Assyrian Captivity
4.4 two
4.5 himself
4.6 a. call
b. promises
4.7 a. Uzziah (Azariah)
b. Jotham
c. Ahaz
d. Hezekiah
4.8 a. Pekah
b. Rezin
4.9 Tabeal
4.10 a. Isaiah
b. Messiah
c. virgin
4.11 Assyria
4.12 a. Assyria
b. Sennacherib
4.13 Either order (b, c):
a. Assyrians
b. Hezekiah
c. Isaiah
4.14 Hezekiah
4.15 a. two
b. 1–35
c. 40–66
4.16 a. conclusion
b. Assyrian
4.17 Babylonian
4.18 a. Jotham
b. Ahaz
c. Hezekiah
4.19 Isaiah
4.20 Judah
4.21 a. Moresheth-gath
b. Jerusalem
c. Gath
4.22 a. born
b. Bethlehem
4.23 a. Samaria
b. Jerusalem
4.24 a. 1:2-2:13
b. 3:1-5:15
c. 6:1-7:20
4.25 a. to do justly
b. to love mercy
c. to walk humbly with God
4.26 true
4.27 false
4.28 false
4.29 true
4.30 false
4.31 a. four
b. Hezekiah
4.32 a. fourth
b. Hezekiah
4.33 a. hidden
b. protected
c. Jehovah
4.34 Deuteronomy
4.35 a. twelfth
b. eighteenth
4.36 a. influence
b. reform
4.37 Judah
4.38 Any order:
a. Philistia
b. Moab
c. Ammon
d. Ethiopia
e. Assyria
4.39 two
4.40 love
4.41 Habakkuk probably prophesied in Judah during the reign of Jehoiakim.
4.42 "The just shall live by faith." (2:4)
4.43 the apparent stay in judgment for the sins of Judah
4.44 Jehovah declared that He was raising up the Chaldeans to judge Judah and that they must rely on Him and live by faith.
4.45 b
4.46 a
4.47 d
4.48 a
4.49 d
4.50 e
4.51 postexilic
4.52 a. I. Messages to Judah 2-45
b. II. Prophecies Against the Nations 46-51

SELF TEST 4

4.01 three
4.02 Israel's failure to obey the voice of God
4.03 first
4.04 a. Asa
b. Hezekiah
c. Josiah
4.05 Babylonian Captivity
4.06 five
4.07 Zedekiah
4.08 Assyria
4.09 true
4.010 false
4.011 true
4.012 true
4.013 false
4.014 b
4.015 e
4.016 a
4.017 d
4.018 c
4.019 Example:
The king's commandments and the priests' responses were according to the divine prescription of the Law of Moses.
4.020 to walk before God in truth with all their hearts and with all their souls
4.021 Example:
God's promise to David by Nathan the prophet concerning an everlasting kingdom was an unconditional promise that would be fulfilled in Christ.
4.022 Any order:
a. to do justly
b. to love mercy
c. to walk humbly with God
4.023 Example:
Jeremiah responded to his prophetic call by saying, "I cannot speak: for I am a child."

LIFEPAC TEST

1. 3
2. 6
3. 8
4. 1
5. 7
6. 4
7. 9
8. 2
9. 5
10. 10
11. Any order:
a. 2 Kings 18-20
b. 2 Chronicles 29-32
c. Isaiah 36-39
12. a. that which was right in the sight of the Lord
b. that David his father did
13. a. sanctify
b. cleanse
14. Assyrians
15. a. rotation
b. earth
16. false
17. true
18. false
19. false
20. true
21. c
22. k
23. g
24. a
25. i
26. f
27. j
28. b
29. h
30. d
31. "Because they obeyed not the voice of the LORD their God, but transgressed his covenant, and all that Moses the servant of the LORD commanded, and would not hear them, nor do them."
32. Example:
God's promise to David by Nathan the prophet concerning an everlasting kingdom was an unconditional promise that would be fulfilled in Christ.

ALTERNATE LIFEPAC TEST

1. b
2. i
3. f
4. k
5. j
6. a
7. g
8. e
9. h
10. c
11. true
12. true
13. false
14. false
15. true
16. true
17. false
18. false
19. true
20. true
21. d
22. a
23. d
24. c
25. b
26. royal
27. Nineveh
28. prison
29. Temple
30. one hundred and thirty-seven
31. Any order:
a. 2 Kings
b. 2 Chronicles
c. Isaiah
32. Any order:
a. Tiglath-pileser
b. Shalmaneser
c. Sargon
d. Sennacherib
33. Any order:
a. Isaiah
b. Micah
c. Nahum
d. Zephaniah
e. Habakkuk
f. Jeremiah
34. Any order:
a. opened the Temple
b. restored worship
c. kept the Passover

BIBLE 1008

ALTERNATE LIFEPAC TEST

NAME ______________________________

DATE ______________________________

SCORE ______________________________

Match these items (each answer, 2 points).

1.	________	Manasseh	a.	did that which was right
2.	________	Pharaoh	b.	became king at age twelve years
3.	________	Jehoahaz	c.	son of Manasseh
4.	________	Zedekiah	d.	son of Zedekiah
5.	________	Jehoiachin	e.	became king at age eight years
6.	________	Hezekiah	f.	reigned three months
7.	________	Jehoiakim	g.	Eliakim
8.	________	Josiah	h.	king of Babylon
9.	________	Nebuchadnezzar	i.	defeated at Carchemish
10.	________	Amon	j.	son of Eliakim
			k.	Mattaniah

Write true or false (each answer, 1 point).

11. ______________ When apostasy reaches its outer limits, divine judgment will be executed.

12. ______________ Asa, Hezekiah, and Josiah were said to do right in the sight of the Lord.

13. ______________ The Lord added twenty years to Hezekiah's life.

14. ______________ Josiah ordered the Tabernacle to be repaired.

15. ______________ Jehoahaz was taken captive by Pharaoh-nechoh.

16. ______________ The alternative to God's promise to David is judgment.

17. ______________ God's promise to David ended with the fall of Judah.

18. ____________ Isaiah was the son of Amos the prophet.

19. ____________ Micah was a contemporary of Isaiah.

20. ____________ Nehushtan was a brazen serpent used as a pagan idol in Judah.

Write the letter for the correct answer on each line (each answer, 2 points).

21. Israel went into captivity because it ____________ .

a. would not obey the Lord
b. transgressed the covenant
c. would not obey the Law
d. a, b, and c

22. Israel was carried into captivity by ____________ .

a. Assyria
b. Judah
c. Egypt
d. Babylon

23. Judah was delivered from Sennacherib's army by ____________ .

a. Isaiah
b. Hezekiah
c. God
d. the angel of the Lord

24. The ambassador to whom Hezekiah showed the treasures of Judah was from ____________ .

a. Egypt
b. Edom
c. Babylon
d. Assyria

25. The prophet Nahum revealed God's judgment upon ____________ .

a. Edom
b. Assyria
c. Judah
d. Babylon

Complete these statements (each answer, 3 points).

26. Zephaniah was of ________________________ lineage.

27. Nahum told of the fall of the city of ________________________ .

28. During the siege of Jerusalem, Jeremiah was in ________________________ .

29. Manasseh placed a carved image in the ________________________ .

30. The kingdom of Judah survived the kingdom of Israel for approximately ________________________ years.

Complete these activities (each answer, 3 points).

31. List the three Old Testament books that record Hezekiah's reign.

a. ____________________

b. ____________________

c. ____________________

32. List the four kings of Assyria mentioned in this LIFEPAC.

a. ____________________ b. ____________________

c. ____________________ d. ____________________

33. List the six writing prophets discussed in this LIFEPAC.

a. ____________________ b. ____________________

c. ____________________ d. ____________________

e. ____________________ f. ____________________

34. List the three major acts of reform accomplished by Hezekiah.

a. ____________________

b. ____________________

c. ____________________

BIBLE 1009

Unit 9: The Captivity

TEACHER NOTES

MATERIALS NEEDED FOR LIFEPAC	
Required	Suggested
• none	• Bible, King James Version • other versions of the Bible if permitted • wall map of the ancient Near East during the sixth century B.C. • Unger's or Halley's Bible handbook • Bible atlas • Bible concordance • Bible dictionary • the reference materials can be in either book or online formats

ADDITIONAL LEARNING ACTIVITIES

Section 1: Jeremiah

1. Josiah cleaned up Judah on the outside but was unable to turn the hearts of the people from their sins. Discuss similar situations today and emphasize the importance of the inward change in man.
2. Discuss how Jeremiah was opposed during his ministry. Consider the possibility that if one speaks the truth, he may encounter opposition. What should we do when we are attacked by others for righteousness sake?
3. Have the students make a time line of the ministry of Jeremiah. Display the time line in the classroom upon completion.
4. Have a group of students practice and perform an oral reading of the book of Lamentations. Have each student in the group practice a certain portion and have the group present the reading for the entire class.
5. Make a chart for classroom display that shows and compares the times, intent, and activities of the ministries of Jeremiah, Ezekiel, and Daniel.
6. Using a chain-reference Bible, make a list of New Testament passages that either cite or refer to Jeremiah's writings.

Section 2: Ezekiel

1. Ezekiel was taken from his comfortable home in Judah and placed into captivity in Babylon. Discuss what his situation would have been like.
2. Discuss the prophecies of the Messiah found in Ezekiel's book. Consider how these prophecies were fulfilled when Christ came to earth to save mankind.
3. Make a time line and various illustrated posters of the life and ministry of Ezekiel. Display the completed projects in the classroom.
4. Have the students discuss what they would have done had they lived in Jerusalem during the deportations. Would they have fought the Chaldeans, fled to Egypt, or gone into captivity?
5. Present an oral reading to the class, using a portion of Ezekiel's prophecy. In the introduction to the reading, give the background and meaning of the passage.
6. Make a list of at least five of the Messianic prophecies found in Ezekiel's prophecy. Find Scripture passages in the New Testament that indicate the fulfillment of these prophecies.

Section 3: Daniel

1. Daniel was a teenager when taken to Babylon, and Jeremiah was called into ministry as a very young man. Discuss how God uses young men and women who desire to serve him.
2. Discuss how Daniel outlived kings and even empires. Consider how God often preserves those who serve Him. Emphasize how Daniel always put the Lord's will first in his life.
3. Have groups of students make various posters of the beasts mentioned in the book of Daniel and identify what nations they represent.
4. Have the students present skits illustrating any portion of the book of Daniel. Have each group write a script, cast the players, and perform the skit for the class.
5. Make a time line chronicling the life and ministry of Daniel.
6. Daniel has been called a unique prophet. Write a paper using Scripture references showing how Daniel and his ministry was different than other prophets in the Old Testament.
7. After completing Self Test 3, the students may write a research paper on one of these Gentile kings:

    Nebuchadnezzar

    Belshazzar

    Antiochus Epiphanes

    Darius

    Cyrus

    Alexander the Great

STUDENT WORKSHEET

The activity on the following page may be reproduced as a student worksheet.

» ANSWER KEY

1.	Nebopolassar	612-605
2.	Nebuchadnezzar	605-562
3.	Marduk	562-560
4.	Neriglissar	560-556
5.	Labashi-Marduk	556
6.	Nabonidus	556-539
7.	Belshazzar	553-539

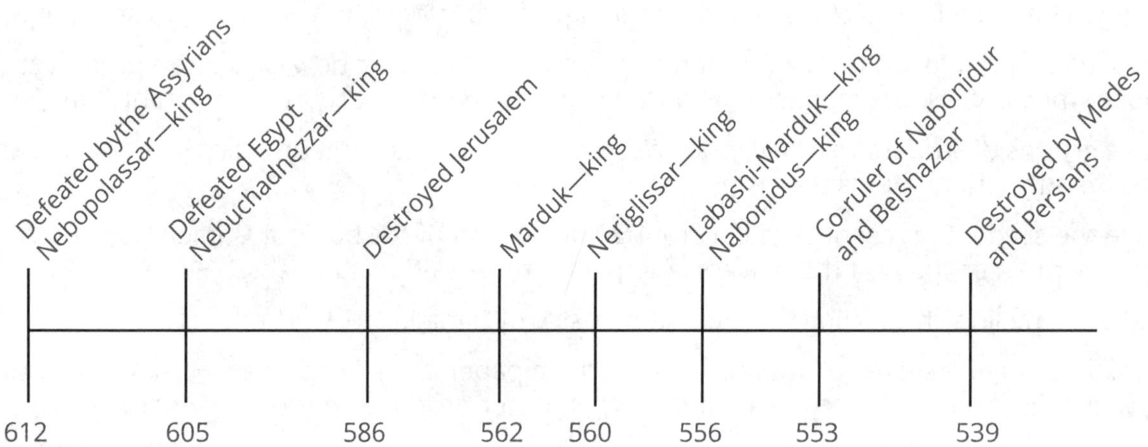

Administer the LIFEPAC Test.
The test is to be administered in one session. Give no help except with directions.
Evaluate the tests and review areas where the students have done poorly.
Review the pages and activities that stress the concepts tested.
If necessary, administer the Alternate LIFEPAC Test.

» THE CHALDEAN EMPIRE AND ITS KINGS

For seventy years, God allowed the Chaldeans to keep His people captive in Babylon. The following list is of the kings of the Chaldean Empire. They are not listed in the correct order. Using additional sources, put these kings in their correct chronological order and find the dates of their reign.

	CORRECT ORDER	DATES
Nebuchadnezzar	1. ______________	______________
Marduk	2. ______________	______________
Labashi-Marduk	3. ______________	______________
Nebopolassar	4. ______________	______________
Belshazzar	5. ______________	______________
Nabonidus	6. ______________	______________
Neriglissar	7. ______________	______________

Using the information you have gained from this activity and the study of the LIFEPAC, make a time line of the Chaldean Empire on this sheet of paper.

ANSWER KEYS

SECTION 1

1.1 true
1.2 false
1.3 true
1.4 true
1.5 false
1.6 true
1.7 false
1.8 true
1.9 true
1.10 true
1.11 a. Anathoth
b. Jerusalem
1.12 being purged and cleansed of apostasy and idolatry
1.13 seek after God
1.14 a. Zephaniah
b. Hezekiah
1.15 a. Temple
b. eighteenth
1.16 irreversibly set
1.17 a. Jehoahaz
b. Jehoiakim
c. Jehoiachin
d. Zedekiah
1.18 Babylonia
1.19 a. Jehoiakim
b. Zedekiah
1.20 a. submit
b. live
c. be punished
1.21 to root out, to pull down, to destroy, to build, to plant
1.22 Example:
God assured Jeremiah that He had made him a "defenced" city, an iron pillar, and a brazen wall. Although the kings, princes, priests, and people would fight against him (God's warning), the Lord was with him to deliver him (God's additional assurance).
1.23 Jeremiah said that Judah was wise to do evil but was without knowledge to do good.
1.24 Example:
Concerning Judah, Jeremiah declared that the poor were oppressed by the rich, the prophets prophesied falsely, and the priests conducted only a profitable ministry. Instead of rejecting the false prophets and mercenary priests, the people approved their wicked ways. Their sacrifices were superficial, and truth had perished in the land.
1.25 Jeremiah warned Judah that they would be subjected by Babylon and that resistance to the divine instrument of judgment would only lead to more severe judgment.
1.26 Jeremiah was arrested and his life was threatened by the prophets, priests, and people.
1.27 Example:
Jehoiakim listened only briefly to the reading of Jeremiah's scroll. Because it predicted the Babylonian Captivity, the scroll was cut into pieces by Jehoiakim and thrown into the fire.
1.28 Jeremiah added to his second scroll the predicted end of Jehoiakim's dynasty and his death.
1.29 Zedekiah
1.30 Example:
Jeremiah prophesied the salvation of Judah and Jerusalem by the "Branch of righteousness" Who would grow out of David and would execute judgment and righteousness in the land.
1.31 a. I. INTRODUCTION 1
b. II. MESSAGES TO JUDAH 2-45
c. III. PROPHECIES AGAINST THE NATIONS 46-51
d. IV. CONCLUSION 52
1.32 duration or length
1.33 a. after
b. Jeremiah
1.34 a. to Jehoiakim's reign
b. of the prophet's personal history
1.35 a. poetic
b. destruction of Jerusalem
1.36 a
1.37 e
1.38 d
1.39 c
1.40 b

SELF TEST 1

1.01 c
1.02 a
1.03 b
1.04 b
1.05 c
1.06 b
1.07 d
1.08 b
1.09 e
1.010 d
1.011 a. prediction
b. duration or length
1.012 poetic description
1.013 his own suffering
1.014 Any order:
a. famine
b. pestilence
c. sword
1.015 Anathoth
1.016 a. Egyptians
b. Babylonians
1.017 Example:
God assured Jeremiah that He had made him a "defenced" city, an iron pillar, and a brasen wall. Although the kings, princes, priests, and people would fight against him (God's warning), the Lord was with him to deliver him (God's additional assurance).
1.018 Example:
Concerning Judah, Jeremiah declared that the poor were oppressed by the rich, the prophets prophesied falsely, and the priests conducted only a profitable ministry. Instead of rejecting the false prophets and mercenary priests, the people approved their wicked ways. Their sacrifices were superficial, and truth had perished in the land.
1.019 Example:
Jeremiah prophesied the salvation of Judah and Jerusalem by the "Branch of righteousness" Who would grow out of David and would execute judgment and righteousness in the land.
1.020 Jeremiah was arrested and his life was threatened by the prophets, priests, and people.
1.021 Example:
Jehoiakim listened only briefly to the reading of Jeremiah's scroll. Because it predicted the Babylonian Captivity, the scroll was cut into pieces by Jehoiakim and thrown into the fire.

SECTION 2

2.1 b
2.2 b
2.3 d
2.4 c
2.5 d
2.6 exile or Babylon
2.7 597
2.8 permitted to live in settlements
2.9 a. Tel-abib
b. Chebar
2.10 a. civil commonwealth
b. word of God from the mouth of His prophet
2.11 e
2.12 f
2.13 a
2.14 d *or* b
2.15 b
2.16 fifth
2.17 captive people
2.18 Thus saith the Lord GOD
2.19 a. repentance
b. restoration for consolation
2.20 a. the fall of Judah
b. the destruction of the Temple and the Holy City
c. the death and deportation of the people
2.21 a. sinfulness
b. holiness
2.22 a. Judah's fall
b. destruction of Jerusalem
2.23 Any order:
a. righteousness
b. justice
c. power
2.24 Any order:
a. Noah
b. Daniel
c. Job
2.25 God of their covenant
2.26 a. I. PROPHECIES OF JUDGMENT 1-24
b II. TRANSITIONAL PROPHECIES 25-32
c. III. PROPHECIES OF MERCY 33-48
2.27 the judgment of God in the destruction of Jerusalem
2.28 to Judah's attempted conspiracy with Egypt against Babylonia
2.29 Whether in His house or not, none shall escape the righteous judgment of God.
2.30 moral and spiritual restoration
2.31 life or autobiography
2.32 idolatry
2.33 burning
2.34 a. lewd adulteress
b. idolatry
2.35 Judah
2.36 after
2.37 Either order:
a. 34
b. 37
2.38 34
2.39 sticks
2.40 coming kingdom

SELF TEST 2

2.01 true
2.02 false
2.03 true
2.04 true
2.05 false
2.06 twelfth
2.07 Anathoth
2.08 Josiah
2.09 Jehoiachin
2.010 Jeremiah
2.011 thirty
2.012 settlements
2.013 holiness of God
2.014 reconcile the nation in exile
2.015 sticks
2.016 a
2.017 d
2.018 b
2.019 e
2.020 c
2.021 Jeremiah said that Judah was wise to do evil but was without knowledge to do good.
2.022 Jeremiah warned Judah that they would be subjected by Babylon and that resistance to the divine instrument of judgment would only lead to more severe judgment.
2.023 the judgment of God in the destruction of Jerusalem
2.024 Example:
Whether in His house or not, none shall escape the righteous judgment of God.
2.025 moral and spiritual restoration

SECTION 3

3.1 false
3.2 true
3.3 true
3.4 false
3.5 true
3.6 605
3.7 Any order:
a. Hananiah
b. Mishael
c. Azariah
3.8 ten
3.9 Belshazzar
3.10 a. three
b. one hundred twenty
3.11 e
3.12 c
3.13 c
3.14 b
3.15 d
3.16 a. a humble heart
b. praise and honor
3.17 second generation successor-grandson
3.18 drinking wine from those vessels and by praising the gods of gold, of silver, of brass, of iron, of wood, and of stone
3.19 fingers of a man's hand to come forth and to write on the wall in the presence of Belshazzar
3.20 the fall of the Babylonian Empire and the end of Belshazzar's reign
3.21 a. first
b. three (over 120 princes)
3.22 thirty
3.23 cast into the den of lions
3.24 law (of Medes and Persians)
3.25 a. God
b. deliver
3.26 cast into the den of lions
3.27 a. living
b. dominion or kingdom
3.28 a. Darius
b. Cyrus
3.29 Any order:
a. God's people in exile
b. the returning remnant
c. believers in every successive era
3.30 outline of their entire future—to the end of the age

3.31 e
3.32 f
3.33 a
3.34 d
3.35 b
3.36 Example:
Daniel wrote not as a member of the community of exiled Jews, but as an officer of the Babylonian state and a chief of their wise men.
3.37 Example:
In the writings of the prophets, God's people usually are assigned the major historical role; however, in Daniel's book, the major historical role is given to the world power that God had raised up to be His instrument of judgment upon His people.
3.38 Like Nebuchadnezzar's forgotten dream, given with its interpretation by God to Daniel in a night vision, Daniel's vision of the four beasts represented the succession of four world kingdoms beginning with Nebuchadnezzar.
3.39 The term *week* in Greek refers not to seven days, but to seven years.
3.40 four hundred eighty-three years after the decree of Cyrus to rebuild Jerusalem

SELF TEST 3

3.01 e
3.02 c
3.03 e
3.04 c
3.05 b
3.06 b
3.07 b
3.08 d
3.09 c
3.010 d
3.011 Nebuchadnezzar
3.012 Nebuchadnezzar
3.013 drinking wine from those vessels and by praising the gods of gold, of silver, of brass, of iron, of wood, and of stone
3.014 fingers of a man's hand to come forth and to write on the wall in the presence of Belshazzar
3.015 the fall of the Babylonian Empire and the end of Belshazzar's reign
3.016 cast into the den of lions
3.017 outline of their entire future—to the end of the age
3.018 law (of the Medes and Persians)
3.019 believers in every successive era
3.020 ten times wiser than all the magicians and astrologers in the domain
3.021 Example:
God assured Jeremiah that He had made him a "defenced" city, an iron pillar, and a brasen wall. Although the kings, princes, priests, and people would fight against him (God's warning), the Lord was with him to deliver him (God's additional assurance).
3.022 moral and spiritual restoration
3.023 Example:
In the writings of the prophets, God's people usually are assigned the major historical role; however, in Daniel's book, the major historical role is given the world power that God had raised up to be His instrument of judgment upon His people.
3.024 The term *week* in Greek refers not to seven days, but to seven years.
3.025 Example:
Like Nebuchadnezzar's forgotten dream given with its interpretation by God to Daniel in a night vision, Daniel's vision of the four beasts represented the succession of four world kingdoms beginning with Nebuchadnezzar.

LIFEPAC TEST

1. a
2. b
3. b
4. b
5. d
6. e
7. f
8. a
9. d *or* b
10. b
11. false
12. true
13. true
14. false
15. true
16. Aramaic
17. hearts
18. being purged and cleansed of idolatry and apostasy
19. a. I. INTRODUCTION 1
    b. II. MESSAGES TO JUDAH 2-45
    c. III. PROPHECIES AGAINST THE NATIONS 46-51
    d. IV. CONCLUSION 52
20. His people in exile or the captives in Babylon
21. Thus saith the Lord GOD
22. the judgment of God in the destruction of Jerusalem
23. Either order:
    a. 34
    b. 37
24. a. 605
    b. Jehoiakim
25. a. I. HISTORY 1-6
    b. II. PROPHECY 7-12
26. Example:
    Jeremiah warned Judah that they would be subjected by Babylon and that resistance to the divine instrument of judgment would only lead to more severe judgment.
27. Example:
    In the writings of the prophets, God's people usually are assigned the major historical role; however, in Daniel's book, the major historical role is given to the world power that God had raised up to be His instrument of judgment upon His people.
28. Example:
    Jeremiah prophesied the salvation of Judah and Jerusalem by the "Branch of righteousness" Who would grow out of David and would execute judgment and righteousness in the land.

ALTERNATE LIFEPAC TEST

1. e
2. c
3. i
4. g
5. k
6. d
7. j
8. f
9. h
10. a
11. false
12. true
13. false
14. false
15. true
16. false
17. true
18. false
19. Branch
20. Hezekiah
21. psalms
22. Jehoiakim
23. priest
24. seventy
25. Gentiles
26. Either order:
    a. Hebrew
    b. Aramaic
27. Either order:
    a. message to Judah
    b. prophecies against nations
28. Either order:
    a. repentance prior to the fall of Jerusalem
    b. ultimate restoration of Judah
29. Any order:
    a. prophecies of judgement
    b. transitional prophecies
    c. prophecies of mercy
30. Either order:
    a. history
    b. prophecy
31. Any order:
    a. Babylon
    b. Media-Persia
    c. Greece
    d. Rome

BIBLE 1009

ALTERNATE LIFEPAC TEST

NAME ______________________

DATE ______________________

SCORE ______________________

Match these items (each answer, 2 points).

1.	________	Zedekiah	a.	son of Amon
2.	________	Jeremiah	b.	Chaldean name of Daniel
3.	________	Belshazzar	c.	chosen before his birth
4.	________	Messiah	d.	placed idols in the Temple
5.	________	Cyrus	e.	revolted against Babylon
6.	________	Manasseh	f.	deported with Jehoiachin
7.	________	Darius	g.	the seed of David
8.	________	Ezekiel	h.	Jeremiah's scribe
9.	________	Baruch	i.	desecrated the Temple vessels
10.	________	Josiah	j.	Median king
			k.	Persian king

Write true or false (each answer, 2 points).

11. ____________ Lamentations is a poetic description of the fall of Babylon.

12. ____________ Jeremiah suffered during the reign of Zedekiah.

13. ____________ Josiah's reforms cleansed the hearts of the people.

14. ____________ Jeremiah did not mention his own suffering in the book of Lamentations.

15. ____________ Ezekiel taught about the Messiah.

16. ____________ Ezekiel did not expect the fall of Judah.

17. ____________ The prophecy of Ezekiel closes with a portrayal of the coming kingdom.

18. ____________ Daniel called the Messiah the little horn of Judah.

Complete these statements (each answer, 3 points).

19. Jeremiah taught that Judah would be saved by the ________________________ of righteousness.

20. Josiah was a fourth-generation descendant of ________________________ .

21. Lamentations includes four major ________________________ .

22. Jeremiah predicted the death of King ________________________ .

23. Ezekiel was born into the family of a ________________________ .

24. The Judeans were in captivity for ________________________ years.

25. Daniel's ministry was primarily to ________________________ .

26. Daniel wrote his prophecy in both a. ________________ and b. ________________ .

Complete these activities (each answer, 3 points).

27. List the two major sections of Jeremiah's prophecy.

    a. ________________________ b. ________________________

28. Write the twofold purpose of Ezekiel's ministry.

    a. ________________________ b. ________________________

29. List the three divisions of Ezekiel's prophecy.

    a. ________________ b. ________________ c. ________________

30. List the two divisions of the prophecy of Daniel.

    a. ________________________ b. ________________________

31. List the nations that the four beasts of Daniel chapter 7 represent.

    a. ________________________ b. ________________________

    c. ________________________ d. ________________________

BIBLE 1010

Unit 10: The Restoration

TEACHER NOTES

MATERIALS NEEDED FOR LIFEPAC	
Required	Suggested
• none	• Bible, King James Version • other versions of the Bible if permitted • wall map of the ancient Near East during the sixth century B.C. • wall map of Jerusalem • Unger's or Halley's Bible handbook • Bible atlas • Bible concordance • Bible dictionary • the reference materials can be in either book or online formats

ADDITIONAL LEARNING ACTIVITIES

Section 1: The First Return from Exile

1. Using God's use of Cyrus as an example, discuss how God can even use the unbeliever to bless the believer. Consider how this situation can occur today in a job, school, or community.
2. Discuss how the return of the Jews to the land ended the period of divine discipline upon God's people. Consider from the Scriptures how this event was a fulfillment of prophecy and a demonstration of God's faithfulness to Israel.
3. Have the students make time lines for display in the classroom that illustrate the Restoration period.
4. Have groups of students make models of the Temple that was rebuilt when the Jews returned to their land.
5. Make maps that trace the return of Jews from Persia to Jerusalem. Display the finished projects in the classroom.
6. Write a brief paper on what part you would have liked to play in the return and the rebuilding of the Temple had you lived during the time of the first return.

Section 2: The Preservation in Exile

1. The book of Esther is the only book of the Bible that does not mention the name of God. One book in the New Testament does not mention the name of Jesus Christ. Give possible reasons for these omissions.
2. Using Esther and other women mentioned in the Bible, discuss how God can use women who seek his will. Identify great women who are mentioned in the Scriptures.
3. Have the students present to the class oral readings of the book of Esther. Select any one portion of the book for the reading. In the introduction to the reading, relate the background of the text.
4. Make a list of women in the Old Testament who were used by God. Include Scripture references in your list.

Section 3: The Second Return From Exile

1. Using Ezra's return as an example, discuss the need for spiritual rebuilding as well as physical rebuilding. Consider how the Jews had rebuilt the physical Temple, but not the temple inside their hearts.
2. Discuss how the reforms of Ezra parallel the reforms of Hezekiah and Josiah. Emphasize the necessity of reform and revival if people are to serve the Lord.
3. Have the students form groups and make charts or posters depicting or outlining the book of Ezra. Display the finished products in the classroom.
4. Discuss the three returns to the land. Have each student select and give reasons for the return he would have liked to have been a part of if he lived during that time.
5. Present an oral reading of any portion of the book of Ezra. In your introduction, give the background information of the passage.
6. Write a 200 word article that might have appeared in a Jerusalem newspaper, describing Ezra's reform and revival.

Section 4: The Third Return from Exile

1. Discuss the importance of spiritual rebuilding. Emphasize that the greatness of a nation rests on its spiritual foundation that will then lead to taking practical steps for safety and preservation.
2. Using a wall map, review the shape, size, and important places in the city of Jerusalem.
3. Have the students form groups and make models of the city of Jerusalem.
4. Have the students form groups to make comparative charts of the three returns to Jerusalem. Display the finished products in the classroom.
5. Write a brief paper comparing the reforms of the book of Nehemiah with the reforms listed in the book of Ezra.
6. Write a brief report on the problems caused by others during the construction of the walls of the city of Jerusalem. Use additional sources.
7. After completing Section 4 of the LIFEPAC, the student may write a research paper on the ministry, life, and impact of either Zerubbabel, Ezra, or Nehemiah. Additional sources should be used and cited within the report.

Section 5: The Prophets of the Period

1. Have the students form teams and read passages of Scripture from Ezra, Nehemiah, Haggai, Zechariah, and Malachi. Have the teams guess from which passage of Scripture each verse comes. Give extra points to the winning team. This game can also be played in "Jeopardy" format.
2. Discuss the importance of the ministry of the prophet in maintaining Israel's spiritual welfare. Parallel this idea to the need Christians have in hearing the Word of God.
3. Have the students make charts comparing the ministries and messages of Haggai, Zechariah, and Malachi.
4. Have the students discuss and list the Messianic prophecies and promises found in the three prophetic books studied in this section.
5. Make a poster illustrating the outline of the books of Haggai, Zechariah, and Malachi. Use additional sources.
6. Using a chain-reference Bible, make a list of the New Testament passages that refer to or quote from the books of Haggai, Zechariah, or Malachi.

STUDENT WORKSHEET

The activity on the following page can be reproduced as a student worksheet.

» ANSWER KEY

1. Obadiah
2. Joel
3. Jonah
4. Hosea
5. Amos
6. Isaiah
7. Micah
8. Nahum
9. Zephaniah
10. Jeremiah
11. Habakkuk
12. Ezekiel
13. Haggai
14. Zechariah
15. Malachi

Theme: Any reasonable answer will meet the requirements of this assignment.

Administer the LIFEPAC Test.

The test is to be administered in one session. Give no help except with directions.
Evaluate the tests and review areas where the students have done poorly.
Review the pages and activities that stress the concepts tested.
If necessary, administer the Alternate LIFEPAC Test.

» THE OLD TESTAMENT PROPHETS

Listed below are the writing prophets of the Old Testament. See if you can list them in their correct chronological order, with the earliest one on line one. Also see if you can identify the theme of the prophecy they wrote. Check your answers and correct any errors.

	CHRONOLOGICAL ORDER	THEME
Obadiah	1. ____________	____________
Jonah	2. ____________	____________
Amos	3. ____________	____________
Micah	4. ____________	____________
Zephaniah	5. ____________	____________
Habakkuk	6. ____________	____________
Zechariah	7. ____________	____________
Joel	8. ____________	____________
Ezekiel	9. ____________	____________
Hosea	10. ____________	____________
Isaiah	11. ____________	____________
Nahum	12. ____________	____________
Jeremiah	13. ____________	____________
Haggai	14. ____________	____________
Malachi	15. ____________	____________

ANSWER KEYS

SECTION 1

1.1 Jeremiah
1.2 seventy
1.3 a. 605
b. 536
1.4 a. all the kingdoms of the earth
b. to build Him a house in Jerusalem
1.5 a. return of the Lord's people to Jerusalem
b. the rebuilding of the Temple
c. the assistance by those remaining
1.6 Temple vessels
1.7 true
1.8 true
1.9 false
1.10 false
1.11 true
1.12 About one in seven
1.13 assistants, musicians (or singers), and porters
1.14 The Nethanims were Temple servants who probably descended from the Gibeonites.
1.15 Jeshua
1.16 Example:
Apparently the high proportion of priests among those people who returned from exile to the Land of Israel did not contribute positively to the spiritual character of the congregation. In Ezra 10:18-19, the sons of the priests were found among those who had sinned by taking foreign wives.
1.17 f
1.18 c
1.19 e
1.20 c
1.21 d
1.22 c
1.23 a
1.24 b
1.25 c
1.26 a
1.27 e

SELF TEST 1

1.01 true
1.02 false
1.03 false
1.04 true
1.05 true
1.06 d
1.07 b
1.08 e
1.09 b
1.010 c
1.011 the reign of Ahasuerus
1.012 offered burnt offerings
1.013 positions of leadership in the work on the house of the Lord
1.014 the foundation of the Temple was laid
1.015 both joy and sorrow
1.016 one of exclusiveness
1.017 stop the work on rebuilding the city of Jerusalem
1.018 the second year of Darius
1.019 completed the house of the Lord
1.020 upon completion of the Temple
1.021 Example:
The Babylonian Captivity began with Nebuchadnezzar's first invasion of Judah in 605 B.C. and ended with King Cyrus's permission to return to the land in 536 B.C.
1.022 Example:
The proclamation of Cyrus permitted the return of the Lord's people to Jerusalem, the rebuilding of the Temple, and the assistance by those remaining in exile with such items as gold, silver, goods, beasts, and freewill offerings.
1.023 Example:
Prior to Cyrus, the Lord had used heathen nations only to judge His people; He used Cyrus, king of Persia, in the restoration of His people and in the rebuilding of His house.
1.024 Example:
The return to the Land of Israel was based completely upon the free choice of each individual exiled family.

1.025 Example:
Apparently the high proportion of priests among those people who returned from exile to the Land of Israel did not contribute positively to the spiritual character of the congregation. In Ezra 10:18-19, the sons of the priests were found among those who had sinned by taking foreign wives.

SECTION 2

2.1 false
2.2 false
2.3 true
2.4 true
2.5 true
2.6 true
2.7 true
2.8 true
2.9 false
2.10 true
2.11 Example:
To go before the king uninvited would violate a law, with the penalty of death, unless the king granted favor by extending his golden scepter to the one approaching his throne.
2.12 Mordecai warned Esther that she would not escape the decree, even in the king's house.
2.13 Examples (either order):
a. Mordecai suggested that if Esther failed to act, deliverance would come to the Jews in some other way even though Esther and her father's house (Mordecai and the descendants of Kish) would surely be destroyed.
b. Mordecai stated that Esther might have been providentially placed in the palace for the salvation of her people.
2.14 Esther requested Mordecai to gather all the Jews of Shushan together for a three-day fast, promising that she and her servants would also fast.
2.15 King Ahasuerus graciously received Esther, extending to her his golden scepter and assuring her that he would grant her any request even to half of his kingdom.
2.16 Esther invited the king and Haman, his chief minister, to a banquet the following day.
2.17 Esther wanted to expose Haman and his plot against her people to King Ahasuerus.
2.18 Haman's wife and friends advised him to construct a gallows and to secure permission from the king to hang Mordecai.
2.19 Haman thought that the honors would be for himself.
2.20 At her banquet when King Ahasuerus was informed by Esther about the plot of Haman against her people, Ahasuerus had Haman hanged on the gallows that Haman had built for Mordecai.

SELF TEST 2

2.01 f
2.02 c
2.03 c
2.04 e
2.05 e
2.06 e
2.07 c
2.08 b
2.09 d
2.010 a
2.011 127
2.012 Ethiopia
2.013 six months
2.014 the wealth and splendor of his kingdom
2.015 the fairest maidens in all the provinces of his kingdom
2.016 one-half century (50 years)
2.017 a descendant of the royal house of the Amalekites
2.018 destroy all the Jews throughout the kingdom of Ahasuerus
2.019 Mordecai's uncle
2.020 Benjamin
2.021 Example:
The return to the Land of Israel was based completely upon the free choice of each individual exiled family.
2.022 Example:
Prior to Cyrus, the Lord had used heathen nations only to judge His people; He used Cyrus, king of Persia, in the restoration of His people and in the rebuilding of His house.
2.023 Example:
To go in before the king uninvited would violate a law with the penalty of death, unless the king granted favor by extending his golden sceptre to the one approaching his throne.
2.024 Esther requested Mordecai to gather all the Jews of Shushan together for a three-day fast, promising that she and her servants would also fast.
2.025 Esther invited the king and Haman, his chief minister, to a banquet the following day.

SECTION 3

3.1 Aaron
3.2 Law of Moses
3.3 hand of the LORD
3.4 a. a letter from King Artaxerxes
b. a register listing the heads of the families that accompanied Ezra to Jerusalem
3.5 for the support of Ezra's mission and ministry
3.6 heart or spiritual
3.7 a. to seek the law of the Lord
b. to do it
c. to teach statutes and judgments in Israel
3.8 free will or choice
3.9 similar
3.10 fast
3.11 Either order:
a. He wanted God's guidance and protection on the way.
b. He wanted their words of faith in God, that they had spoken to the king, confirmed.
3.12 to the priests
3.13 four months
3.14 approximately fifty years
3.15 a knowledge of the Law of God and a faithful application of that Law in their daily lives
3.16 false
3.17 true
3.18 true
3.19 true
3.20 false
3.21 a. his garments or clothes
b. his hair and beard
3.22 Any order:
a. people
b. priests
c. Levites
3.23 Jerusalem
3.24 cut off
3.25 As thou hast said, so must we do

SELF TEST 3

3.01 true
3.02 true
3.03 true
3.04 false
3.05 false
3.06 true
3.07 true
3.08 true
3.09 false
3.010 false
3.011 ready scribe
3.012 volunteers
3.013 heart or spiritual
3.014 family names
3.015 fast
3.016 priests
3.017 four months
3.018 fifty
3.019 a. priests
b. righteousness or all things
3.020 a. to seek the law of the Lord
b. to do it
c. to teach statutes and judgments in Israel
3.021 Either order:
a. He wanted God's guidance and protection on the way.
b. He wanted their words of faith in God that they had spoken to the king confirmed.
3.022 a knowledge of the Law of God and a faithful application of that Law in their daily lives
3.023 Examples:
a. Modecai suggested that if Esther failed to act, deliverance would come to the Jews in some other way even though Esther and her father's house (Mordecai and the descendants of Kish) would surely be destroyed.
b. Mordecai stated that Esther might have been providentially placed in the palace for the salvation of her people.
3.024 Example:
Apparently the high proportion of priests among those people who returned from exile to the Land of Israel did not contribute positively to the spiritual character of the congregation. In Ezra 10:18-19, the sons of the priests were found among those who had sinned by taking foreign wives.

SECTION 4

4.1 b
4.2 d
4.3 d
4.4 a
4.5 d
4.6 Hanani
4.7 Either order (a, b):
a. affliction
b. reproach
c. walls
d. gates
4.8 to send him to Jerusalem that he might build it
4.9 How long will your journey be?
When will you return?
4.10 Nehemiah requested letters to provincial governors for protection along the way and for provision of building materials upon his arrival in Jerusalem.
4.11 c
4.12 a
4.13 b
4.14 true
4.15 true
4.16 true
4.17 false
4.18 true
4.19 false
4.20 true
4.21 a. land
b. children
c. food
d. taxes
4.22 a. walk in the fear of God
b. his own example of sacrificial work and generosity
4.23 Any order:
a. They invited Nehemiah to come to them and talk, planning to harm him.
b. They circulated a letter containing false accusations against Nehemiah.
c. They hired prophets to persuade Nehemiah to flee to the Temple for refuge.
4.24 fifty–two
4.25 wrought of (or accomplished by) God
4.26 genealogies
4.27 be enrolled by genealogies
4.28 a. Hebrew congregation
b. priests and Levites
c. line by which the promised Redeemer would come

4.29 excluded from the priesthood
4.30 a. 7
b. 2
4.31 a. water
b. morning
c. midday
4.32 stood and worshipped God
4.33 Tabernacles
4.34 a. confession
b. repentance or separation from sin
4.35 covenant
4.36 Either order (b, c):
a. Nehemiah
b. priests
c. Levites
4.37 one tenth
4.38 dedication
4.39 a. purified
b. priests
4.40 a. Tobiah
b. Sanballat's

SELF TEST 4

4.01 false
4.02 true
4.03 false
4.04 false
4.05 true
4.06 affliction and reproach
4.07 he might build it
4.08 provision of building materials upon his arrival in Jerusalem
4.09 priests
4.010 within and outside the congregation
4.011 sheep
4.012 they were "outside" gates
4.013 inside gates, which belonged to the Temple and palace units
4.014 a weapon in one hand and worked with the other
4.015 the walls had been wrought of (accomplished by) God
4.016 a. walk in the fear of God
b. his own example of sacrificial work and generosity
4.017 Nehemiah prayed to the God of heaven and spoke to the king
4.018 Examples (any order):
a. They invited Nehemiah to come to them and talk, planning to harm him.
b. They circulated a letter containing false accusations against Nehemiah.
c. They hired prophets to persuade Nehemiah to flee to the Temple for refuge.
4.019 Example:
Prior to Cyrus, the Lord had used heathen nations only to judge His people; He used Cyrus, king of Persia, in the restoration of His people and in the rebuilding of His house.
4.020 Examples:
a. Mordecai suggested that if Esther failed to act, deliverance would come to the Jews in some other way even though Esther and her father's house (Mordecai and the descendants of Kish) would surely be destroyed.
b. Mordecai stated that Esther might have been providentially placed in the palace for the salvation of her people.
4.021 a. to seek the Law of the Lord
b. to do it
c. to teach statutes and judgments in Israel
4.022 c *or* d
4.023 a
4.024 b

SECTION 5

5.1 a. Ezra
b. Nehemiah
c. Esther
5.2 a. Zerubbabel
b. 536
5.3 a. Ezra
b. 458
5.4 a. Nehemiah
b. 445
5.5 a. Haggai
b. Zechariah
c. Malachi
5.6 a. seventh
b. first
5.7 a. second
b. second
5.8 despondency
5.9 a. their original enthusiasm for rebuilding the house of the Lord
b. more interested in their private homes and their own personal concerns
5.10 a. Temple
b. people of God
5.11 four
5.12 b
5.13 d
5.14 a
5.15 c
5.16 Haggai
5.17 a. priests
b. Zerubbabel
5.18 a. two
b. Haggai
5.19 the future of the covenant people and the Messianic kingdom
5.20 four
5.21 f
5.22 e
5.23 c
5.24 a
5.25 d
5.26 postexilic
5.27 Malachi condemned the same sins that Nehemiah had found.
5.28 Any order:
a. priestly indifference and defilements
b. neglect of the tithes
c. mixed marriages with non–Jews
d. failure to keep the Sabbath
5.29 God's love for Israel
5.30 destiny of the righteous and the wicked

SELF TEST 5

5.01 true
5.02 true
5.03 false
5.04 false
5.05 false
5.06 Esther
5.07 returned to Jerusalem with Zerubbabel
5.08 one in seven
5.09 praised the Lord with musical instruments and song
5.010 word of the Lord by Haggai the prophet
5.011 India to Ethiopia
5.012 a descendant of the royal house of the Amalekites
5.013 Chapters 6 and 7 of Ezra
5.014 a skilled, learned scholar in the Law of Moses
5.015 a weapon in one hand
5.016 e
5.017 a
5.018 f
5.019 d
5.020 c
5.021 a. to seek the Law of the Lord
b. to do it
c. to teach statutes and judgements in Israel
5.022 Any order:
a. priestly indifference and defilements
b. neglect of the tithes
c. mixed marriages with non-Jews
d. failure to keep the Sabbath
5.023 Example:
They seemed to have lost their original enthusiasm for rebuilding the house of the Lord, and they became more interested in their private homes and personal concerns.
5.024 Example:
for the future of the covenant people and the Messianic kingdom.
5.025 Example:
The return to the Land of Israel was based completely upon the free choice of each individual exiled family.

LIFEPAC TEST

1. true
2. false
3. true
4. true
5. false
6. reconstructed the altar, and offered burnt offerings
7. positions of leadership in the work on the house of the Lord
8. the wealth and splendor of his kingdom
9. a descendant of the royal house of the Amalekites
10. ready scribe
11. he might build it
12. within and outside the congregation
13. the walls had been wrought of (accomplished by) God
14. the future of the covenant people and the Messianic kingdom
15. praised the Lord with musical instruments and song
16. d
17. a
18. c
19. e
20. f
21. b
22. e
23. d
24. e
25. b
26. a. to seek the Law of the Lord
    b. to do it
    c. to teach statutes and judgments in Israel
27. Example:
    The Babylonian Captivity began with Nebuchadnezzar's first invasion of Judah in 605 B.C. and ended with King Cyrus's permission to return to the land in 536 B.C.
28. Example:
    They seemed to have lost their original enthusiasm for rebuilding the house of the Lord, and they became more interested in their private homes and personal concerns.

ALTERNATE LIFEPAC TEST

1. d
2. i
3. f
4. k
5 b
6. h
7. e
8. j
9. g
10. c
11. true
12. true
13. false
14. true
15. false
16. false
17. false
18. true
19. true
20. true
21. seventh
22. Passover
23. Jews
24. Shushan
25. Ezra
26. intermarrying
27. a weapon
28. Temple
29. night
30. Nehemiah
31. a. 536 B.C.
    b. 458 B.C.
    c. 445 B.C.

BIBLE 1010

ALTERNATE LIFEPAC TEST

NAME ______________________

DATE ______________________

SCORE ______________________

Match these items (each answer, 2 points).

1.	________	Artaxerxes	a.	first prophet
2.	________	Nehemiah	b.	returned the Temple vessels to the Jews
3.	________	Esther	c.	Sheshbazzar
4.	________	Malachi	d.	ordered a halt to the Temple building
5.	________	Cyrus	e.	Vashti's husband
6.	________	Ezra	f.	Mordecai's cousin
7.	________	Ahasuerus	g.	an Agagite
8.	________	Zechariah	h.	a scribe
9.	________	Haman	i.	of the tribe of Judah
10.	________	Zerubbabel	j.	contemporary of Haggai
			k.	last of the Old Testament prophets

Write true or false (each answer, 2 points).

11. ____________ God made Cyrus the greatest king in the world.

12. ____________ The Temple was completed in the ninth year of Darius.

13. ____________ The royal festival of Ashasuerus lasted for six months.

14. ____________ The feast of Purim observes God's deliverance of His people at the time of Esther.

15. ____________ Ezra required that the people pay money to remove their sin.

16. ____________ The people of Israel fought against Ezra's reforms.

17. ____________ Sanballat and Tobiah helped rebuild Jerusalem's walls.

18. ____________ Revival occurred in Jerusalem as Ezra read the Word.

19. ____________ Haggai ministered while Darius was king.

20. ____________ Zechariah wrote of the coming Messianic kingdom.

Complete these statements (each answer, 3 points).

21. Burnt offerings were sacrificed unto the Lord in the ________________ month after the first return.

22. When the Temple was completed, the people celebrated the feast of ________________ .

23. Haman persuaded Ahasuerus to destroy the ________________ .

24. The capital city of the Persian Empire was ________________ .

25. The second return to the land was lead by ________________ .

26. The new congregation in Jerusalem sinned by ________________ with the heathen.

27. The Jews who worked on the wall worked with one hand and held ________________ in the other.

28. All of Haggai's prophecy deals specifically with the ________________ .

29. Zechariah's prophecy included eight ________________ visions.

30. Some scholars believe that Malachi and ________________ were contemporaries.

Complete this activity (each answer, 3 points).

31. List the dates of the following returns of the Jews to Jerusalem.

    a. First return ____________________

    b. Second return ____________________

    c. Third return ____________________